The Childbearing Year

Barbara B. Holstein

NEW READERS PRESS

Publishing Division of Laubach Literacy International
Syracuse, New York

**Dedicated to the good health of
mothers and babies
everywhere**

ISBN 0-88336-567-7

© 1990
New Readers Press
Publishing Division of
Laubach Literacy International
Box 131, Syracuse, New York 13210

Printed in the United States of America

Editor: Teddy Norwich Kempster
Editorial Assistant: Elizabeth Costello
Design: Chris Steenwerth and Joanne Groth
Illustrations by Nancy Muncy Rhodes
Cover Photo: Hal Silverman/Hal Silverman Studio

9   8   7   6   5   4   3   2

Table of Contents

To the Reader:

This book is about having a baby. It is about pregnancy. It is about birth. Most women have many questions about birth. I hope this book answers a lot of your questions.

There is much to learn about having a baby. One book cannot tell you all you need to know. Talk to your nurses. Talk to your doctor. Ask them lots of questions.

Learn all you can about birth. Learn all you can about new babies. Learn all you can so that you can make good decisions— for yourself and for your baby.

Knowledge is power.

Good luck!

Barbara Holstein

Barbara B. Holstein

To the Teacher:

This book touches on many of the areas childbirth educators feel are most important in the preparation of women for childbirth and early parenting. It is designed to supplement your other instructional materials and aims at actively involving women in prepared childbirth.

The physical and emotional health of a mother during the childbearing year is of great importance to the health of her child. Throughout the book, mothers are encouraged to take responsibility for themselves—to take care of their bodies, their minds, and their babies. They are encouraged to trust and talk to their health care providers. It will be your role to respond to their questions by offering information, support, and caring.

Each chapter begins with a list of key words that might not be familiar to the reader. These words and other basic terms are defined in the glossary on page 97.

This book cannot and does not claim to provide exhaustive information about pregnancy, childbirth, and early parenting. It does attempt to provide a clear, broad picture of what is happening to the mother and developing baby, and what to expect along the way. The questions and answers included in many of the chapters should provoke other questions and discussion. The narrative comments by three "real" expectant mothers add realistic feelings and experiences to consider during discussion.

Writing activities range from preparing for questions likely to be asked by the prenatal-care provider to analysis of nutritional habits to brief accounts of personal feelings. You might suggest to the women you are working with that they keep a journal to record events of interest during their pregnancy as well as their feelings, fears, and questions. They could keep a page for questions to ask the doctor at prenatal visits.

Above all, keep encouraging them to be active participants in the process of preparing for childbirth and parenting.

Meet Three Mothers

In this book, three women will talk about having a baby. Each one is different, just as you are. They are not the women whose pictures you see here, but their stories are just as true.

Meet Maria:

My name is Maria. I have three other kids. This one was a surprise.

Meet Kim:

My name is Kim. I'm 26. This is my first baby. I'm very excited.

Meet Cindy:

My name is Cindy. I'm 16. Having a baby at 16 isn't easy.

Chapter 1
First Things First

Word Guide

alcohol	pregnant	protein
caffeine	prenatal care	vitamins

Are you going to have a baby? If you are pregnant, you have three things to do:
1. Take care of your body.
2. Take care of your mind.
3. Take care of your baby before it is born.

Take care of your body

Is this your first baby? Have you had other babies?

In either case, the best thing you can do is take care of your body. Here's how:
- Go to the doctor.
- Eat good food.
- Stay away from cigarettes, alcohol, and drugs.

Go to the doctor

If you don't have a doctor, go to a clinic. Ask for prenatal care. *Prenatal* means "before birth." Regular prenatal checkups keep you and your baby healthy. You'll read more about going to the doctor in chapter 2.

If you think you are pregnant, go to your doctor or clinic as soon as possible.

Eat good food

Good food keeps you healthy. It helps keep your baby healthy, too. Eating well will help give your baby a good start.

Think about your eating habits. These questions will help you.

1. **What meals do you eat?**
   - ☐ breakfast
   - ☐ lunch
   - ☐ dinner
   - ☐ snacks
   - ☐ I skip a lot of meals.
   - ☐ I eat when someone else cooks.

2. **Do you eat a lot of:**
   - ☐ french fries
   - ☐ cereals, breads
   - ☐ cakes, cookies, pies
   - ☐ potato chips
   - ☐ candy, chocolate bars
   - ☐ raw fruits and vegetables

3. **How much salt do you use?**
   - ☐ no salt
   - ☐ a little salt
   - ☐ a lot of salt

4. **Which foods do you eat the most?**
   - ☐ beans and rice
   - ☐ burgers and fries
   - ☐ fresh fruits and vegetables
   - ☐ T.V. dinners and frozen pizza
   - ☐ chicken, fish, turkey
   - ☐ ham, hot dogs, salami

5. **What do you drink?**
   - ☐ soda
   - ☐ coffee or tea
   - ☐ fruit juice
   - ☐ milk or milk products
   - ☐ water
   - ☐ wine or beer

What did you learn about yourself?
- Do you eat regular meals?
- Do you eat a variety of foods?
- Is what you eat good for you and your baby?

You need to eat food that's good for you and your baby. Choose food from each of the four basic food groups every day. These four groups are:
- milk and milk products
- grains
- protein products
- fruits and vegetables

Protein products
2 servings a day

Fruits and vegetables
4 servings a day ▶

When you go to the doctor or clinic, ask for help in choosing good foods.

It's good to eat:

fruits and vegetables	fresh chicken and turkey
breads and cereals	fish
cheese	nuts
eggs	beans

But some foods have a lot of fat and salt. They're not good for you or your baby.

Eat as little as possible of these:

ham	chips, french fries
hot dogs	frozen foods
salami	

It's good to drink:
water
milk and milkshakes
juices

Some drinks have caffeine. Too much caffeine can hurt your baby.

Drink as little as possible of these:
coffee
tea
soda

▲ Milk and milk products
4 servings a day

Grains (Whole grain is best.)
4 servings a day ▼

Tips for healthy eating:
- Wash your hands before you cook.
- Wash all fruits and vegetables.
- Do not eat raw meat.
- Do not share your food with your pets.
- Put food that you do not eat into the refrigerator. Do not let food sit out on the table all day.

Stay away from cigarettes, alcohol, and drugs

What you put in your body goes into your baby's body.

Don't smoke. Smoking is bad for you. It is worse for your baby. If you smoke half a pack of cigarettes a day, it can make your baby very sick.

Don't drink alcohol. No one knows how much alcohol is safe when you're pregnant.

Don't use illegal drugs. Cocaine, heroin, crack, PCP, marijuana, LSD, magic mushrooms—you name it. They will hurt your baby.

Any drug—legal or illegal—may hurt your baby. Talk to your doctor before you take any medicine—even aspirin.

Take care of your mind

Having a baby will change your life. Being pregnant can make a woman feel happy or sad. Planning for a baby can be fun. It can feel scary, too. It can be both at the same time.

Being pregnant can make you feel good, or sick, or lonely. The best way to take care of your mind is to learn. Learn all you can. Learn about birth. Learn about babies.

Here are three ways to learn:
1. **Read books.** Go to the library. There are many books about birth and babies.
2. **See movies.** You can see movies or videos about birth and babies. They may have videos at the clinic or at the library.
3. **Talk to people.** Talk to people who care about you. Talk about your feelings. No one can have a baby all alone. Talk to other mothers. Ask them about birth. Ask them how to take care of a new baby. Mothers know a lot!

Take care of your baby before it is born

The best way to take care of your baby before it is born is to take care of yourself. Go to the doctor. Eat good food.

Start planning

The next thing to do is plan for the baby. Start thinking about how you will take care of the baby. Start planning. Start getting ready to be a mother.

Here are some questions to help you plan. Don't worry if you don't know all the answers.

1. Where do you live now? _____

   Where will you live after your baby is born?

   _____

2. How do you get money to live? _____

   How will you get money to live after your baby is born?

   _____

3. Do you go to school? _____

   Will you go to school after your baby is born? _____

   Who will care for your baby when you go to school?

   _____

4. Do you work? _____

   Will you go back to work after your baby is born? _____

   Who will care for your baby when you go back to work?

   _____

5. Do you have other children? _____

   Will a new baby change things for them? _____

   _____

6. Do you use drugs, smoke, or drink? _____

   Can you stop using drugs, smoking, or drinking? _____

   _____

© 1989 Jeffrey High/Image Productions

The baby's father is important, too

Most healthy moms have healthy babies. Having a healthy daddy helps, too.

Talk to the baby's dad. Ask him about his health. Does he have any health problems? They can affect your baby. Tell your doctor about any health problems.

Find out if there are people in his family with health problems. Find out if there are people in his family with learning problems. Their problems could be your baby's problems, too.

Having a baby is the most important thing two people can do. Do the best you can to give your baby a healthy start.

Maria talks:

I know a lot about babies. I guess I'm an old hand at this. When I'm pregnant, I give up all my bad habits. I think that's why my kids are so healthy.

Kim talks:

I really want to be a mom. I still smoke cigarettes, but I am trying to quit. I'm down to two or three a day.

Cindy talks:

I feel happy but scared, too. At first my boyfriend was mad. Now he is sort of happy. I don't know if he will stay with me. I'm staying in school for now. I like my teachers, and talking to them helps.

Questions and answers about being pregnant

When I am pregnant will I get fat?

Pregnant women gain weight, but you do not have to get fat. You will gain a few pounds every month. You should gain 24 to 34 pounds. You must gain weight to have a healthy baby.

When will I look pregnant?

After four or five months you will look pregnant. Then you will "show."

What do I wear?

In the beginning your regular clothes will fit. After a few months, your clothes will feel too small. Then it's time for maternity clothes. You can borrow maternity clothes. You can buy them. You can also make them.

Can I get my hair done?

Yes. When you look good, you feel good. For color or a perm, check with your doctor.

Will my hair fall out now?

No, your hair will not fall out. Eat good food. Take your vitamins. Wash your hair. Keep it shiny and clean.

Can I get sick if I play with my cat?

Playing with a cat is OK. But do not clean out the litter box. Some cats carry a disease called *toxoplasmosis*. It can make your baby very sick.

Can I go to work?

Yes. Tell your doctor where you work. Tell your doctor what you do.

Can I play games?

Yes! Have fun. Play. Run. Swim. Dance. Play tennis. Ride your bike. If you start to bleed, or if you have bad cramps in your belly, call the doctor.

Can I go to school?

If you are a teenager, it is important to stay in school. Some girls stay in their own schools. Some girls go to special classes for pregnant girls. Talk to your teacher or social worker about the best school for you.

Can I take a bath?

Yes, you can take baths or showers. Bath water cannot get inside you. It cannot hurt the baby.

Chapter 2
Prenatal Care

Hal Silverman/Hal Silverman Studio

If you think you are pregnant, make an appointment at the doctor's office or clinic. You and your baby need good care as soon as possible. Your regular doctor may take care of you. But most often, you will go to a specialist called an obstetrician. An obstetrician has special training to help women during pregnancy and birth. In a clinic or hospital, this department is often called "OB."

Don't worry. Pregnancy is not a sickness. Most pregnant women are healthy. So are their babies.

So why go to the doctor? Your body will be going through many changes. You need to understand them. You need to know the best ways to take care of yourself and your baby.

Good prenatal care can prevent many problems. The earlier you get it, the better. Before you even feel the baby inside you, that baby is growing—and growing fast. Good prenatal care will help your baby have a good start in life.

Your first appointment at the doctor's office

What happens

This is what happens during your first appointment:

- The nurse will weigh you. She will check your blood pressure. She will ask for a urine sample. She may take a blood sample.

- The nurse or doctor will ask you about your health. This will help them take care of any problems. Don't be afraid. Answer the questions. Tell the truth. If you are sick, or worried about your health, tell the doctor.

- The nurse or doctor will give you a general exam. They will check your heart, lungs, eyes, ears, throat, and breasts.

- You will have a pelvic exam. It won't hurt. Try to relax.

  You may have had a pelvic exam before. It's also called an internal exam. The doctor looks into your vagina. He looks at your cervix. He feels to find out how big your uterus (womb) is.

  (For more about your body and what the doctor will check, turn to pages 90 and 91.)

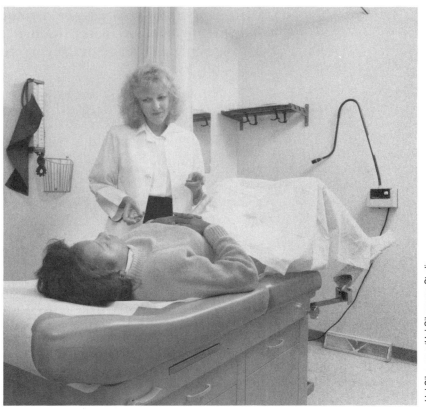

It helps to relax during the pelvic exam. Ask the doctor or nurse to explain what is happening.

Your health history

Knowing about your past health helps your doctor give you the best care now. These are the kinds of questions you will be asked. Answering them now will help you get ready for the first appointment.

Your Health History

How old are you? _____

Is this your first pregnancy? _____

Do you have other children? _____

How much do you weigh? _____

When was your last period? _____

Are your periods regular? _____

Are you using any drugs or medicines?	☐ yes	☐ no
Do you drink wine, beer, or other cocktails?	☐ yes	☐ no
Do you feel healthy?	☐ yes	☐ no
Did you ever have the German measles (rubella) or chicken pox?	☐ yes	☐ no
Do you or does anyone in your family have diabetes? (Some people call diabetes "sugar disease.")	☐ yes	☐ no
Do you or does your mother have high blood pressure?	☐ yes	☐ no
Have you ever had a sexually transmitted disease (STD, a venereal disease, the clap)?	☐ yes	☐ no
Are there people in your family who are sick?	☐ yes	☐ no

What are they sick with? _____

_____

_____

Your due date

When did you have your last period? Knowing this will give you a good idea of when your baby will be born. Pregnancy lasts about nine months. That's about 40 weeks or 280 days.

My last period was _____
                                          (date)

Count back three months: _____

Add seven days: _____

Your due date: _____

Your next appointment

Prenatal care means regular checkups. If you are pregnant, you should go to the doctor once a month. Near the end of pregnancy, you may go more often.

Before you leave your doctor's office, you should set the date and time of your next appointment. You will get an appointment card. Look at it carefully.

```
_____

         HAS AN APPOINTMENT ON
_____
         Day       Month        Date
   AT  _____ A.M. _____ P.M.
```

Be sure to check the date and the time. Will you be at work? Will you be in school? Will you need a ride? Do you want the baby's father to go, too? Do you want your mother or a friend to go with you? Would it be better if they baby-sat your other children?

If you can't go to your appointment, call the office. Make another appointment. When you get prenatal care, your baby does, too!

Maria talks:

I hate dragging the kids to the clinic. I try to go when the big ones are in school. Sometimes it doesn't work out. I try to call if I can't make it.

Cost of care

Prenatal care can cost a lot of money. If you need help to pay bills, tell the people at the clinic. You can pay the bills with:
- cash
- Medicaid
- insurance like Blue Cross
- special maternal-infant care programs in your state
- welfare or public assistance

Here are some things to take with you if you apply for public assistance:
- your Social Security number
- a statement from your doctor that says you are pregnant
- a rent book or a statement of how much rent you owe each month
- your pay stub if you or your baby's father are working

Questions and answers about prenatal care

Why do they want a urine sample?

It tells a lot about your health. It shows if you have a kidney or bladder infection, or if you have signs of diabetes. Diabetes can mean problems for your baby. But it can be treated, and your baby will be safer.

Why do they take a blood sample?

It tells your blood type. It tells if you need more iron. It gives the doctor important facts about your health.

Why do they need to know how much I weigh?

They will keep track of how much you gain and how fast you gain. A sudden weight gain could mean problems.

Why do they take my blood pressure?

Your blood pressure is a sign of your general health during pregnancy. High blood pressure is a danger sign.

What is a pelvic exam for?

The doctor checks for signs of infection or disease. She checks the size of the uterus. It's all part of making sure you and your baby are healthy.

My doctor said I need an ultrasound. What is an ultrasound?

An ultrasound shows where the baby is inside you. The ultrasound machine uses sound waves. It gives a picture of how the baby is growing. The picture is called a sonogram.

My friend told me about a midwife. What does a midwife do?

A midwife helps a woman during pregnancy and birth. She has special training and gives normal prenatal care. Many midwives are also nurses. Most work with doctors.

I'm worried about AIDS.

Everyone is worried about AIDS. If you think you have AIDS, or may have been exposed to AIDS, tell your doctor right away. You can have a blood test to make sure. Talk to the doctor or nurse about AIDS. Find out the best ways to protect yourself.

Can I go to the dentist now?

Yes. Tell the dentist you are pregnant. If you need X rays, they can take special care to protect your baby.

The doctor said I shouldn't take medicine. But if I have a headache, can I take aspirin?

No. Do not take any medicine. If you are sick, call the doctor.

What if I get a bad cold?

Do not take any medicine. If you are sick, call the doctor.

Chapter 3
The First Three Months

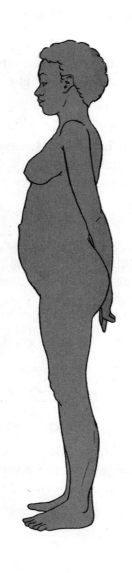

Word Guide			
amniotic sac	hormones	nourishment	trimester
cervix	miscarriage	placenta	umbilical cord
embryo	navel	plug of mucus	

Pregnancy usually lasts for nine months. It is like a long story. In the beginning, everything is new. In the middle, it is interesting. At the end, it is very exciting! In nine months your baby grows and changes. So do you.

The first three months of pregnancy are called the first trimester. A trimester is a period of three or about three months.

What is happening to me?

Your body

At first you do not look pregnant. But soon your body will start to change.

Hormones tell your body to change. Hormones are special chemicals in your body. They tell your body that you are pregnant. They tell your body to send blood and nourishment to the tiny baby. They tell the uterus to grow. They tell your breasts to grow. Your breasts get ready to make milk.

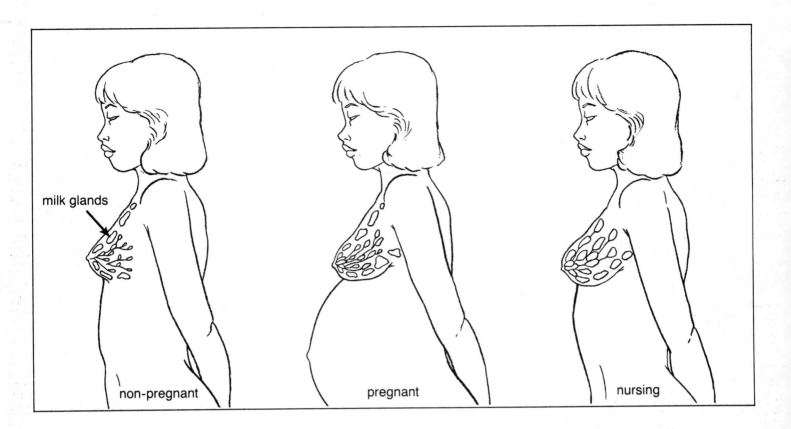

milk glands

non-pregnant

pregnant

nursing

When you are pregnant, your breasts get ready to make milk. The milk glands get larger. The nipples get bigger and darker. By the time your baby is born, your breasts are ready for nursing (breast-feeding).

Your feelings

Some women think being pregnant is great. They are happy. They want to have a baby. They know they will keep the baby.

Some women think being pregnant is not so great. They are not so happy. They do not want to have a baby. They do not know if they will keep the baby.

If you are not happy about being pregnant, it is good to talk about it. Talk to your doctor or your nurse or midwife. Talk to the baby's father. Talk to your teacher or social worker. You may want to talk with them about having an abortion. (Some women choose to have an abortion.)

Some women decide to give the baby up for adoption. It is a big decision. It is not easy. People will help you. In the end, you are the one who must decide.

> ### Cindy talks:
>
> *At first I felt really tired. All I wanted to do was sleep. Sometimes I got scared about what was going to happen to my life. Because I didn't look pregnant, sometimes I pretended I wasn't.*

The first three months

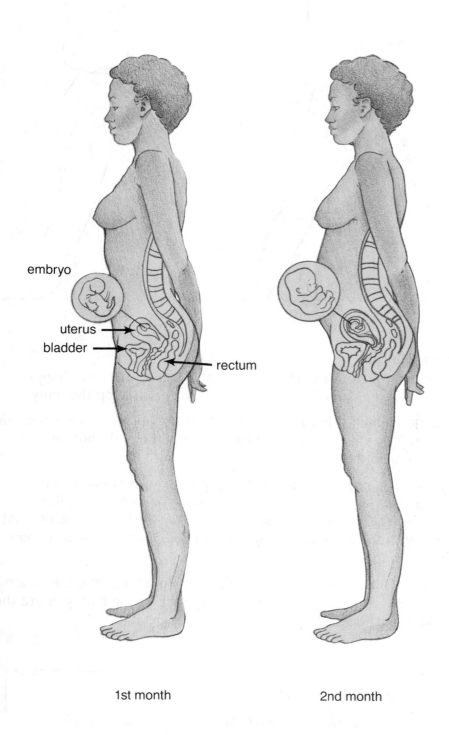

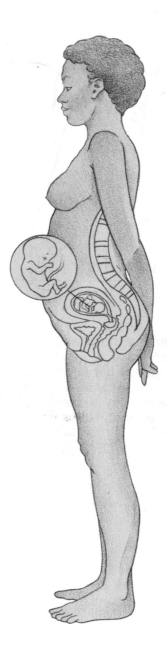

embryo

uterus

bladder

rectum

1st month   2nd month   3rd month

The embryo is too small to see for many weeks. At the end of three months, it is still tiny, and weighs only about three and a half ounces. You won't start to look pregnant until at least the fourth month. ◄

What is happening to my baby?

For the first three months, the tiny baby is called an embryo. *Embryo* means "young one."

The embryo looks like a tiny fish. Soon it has a head. Soon it has tiny arms and legs. Soon a tiny heart starts to beat.

The baby grows inside your uterus. Three things keep the baby safe inside you.

1. A plug of mucus closes the cervix, the opening to the uterus. No more sperm can get into the uterus.

2. The placenta grows. The placenta is attached to the inside of your uterus. It looks like a shiny pancake. The baby is attached to the placenta with the umbilical cord. The baby gets its nourishment through the umbilical cord.

   The place where the baby is attached to the umbilical cord is the navel. Everyone has a navel. It is your belly button.

3. Inside the uterus, the baby lives in a bag of clean, warm water. This is called the amniotic sac. It is also called the bag of waters.

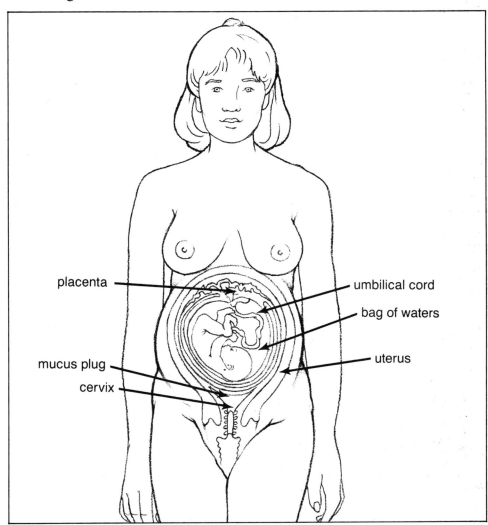

The baby is protected inside the uterus from the beginning. The uterus stretches to fit the growing baby—shown here in the last trimester. ►

27

Some problems in the first trimester

Miscarriage

Sometimes pregnancies end before they are supposed to. The mother does not carry the baby until it can live on its own. This is called a miscarriage. Most miscarriages happen in the first trimester.

A miscarriage can happen fast or it can happen slowly. Sometimes a miscarriage is like having a heavy period.

You may be having a miscarriage if:
- you have bad cramps
- you find blood on your panties or in the toilet
- the blood is thick and lumpy

If you think you are having a miscarriage call the doctor, or go to the hospital or clinic.

A miscarriage usually means something was wrong from the beginning. But it doesn't mean that you won't have a normal pregnancy the next time.

> ### *Maria talks:*
>
> *The first time I got pregnant, I had a miscarriage. I felt scared when it started. Afterwards, I felt sad.*

Morning sickness

Some women feel sick during the first trimester. Some throw up in the morning. This is called morning sickness. If you have morning sickness, keep crackers near your bed. Have a few before you get up in the morning.

Some women feel sick at night. Some feel sick all the time. Feeling sick is not fun. It may help to eat small meals. Eat whenever you feel hungry. Tell the doctor if you throw up all day.

Usually, women feel better when the first trimester is over.

> ### *Kim talks:*
>
> *I felt like throwing up morning, noon, and night. The doctor said it would probably pass, and it did.*

Questions and answers about the first trimester

Can I eat spicy food?

You should always eat good food. If you like spicy food, you can eat it. If it makes you feel sick, do not eat it. Be careful to limit salt.

Can I still make love?

Sex is OK during pregnancy. It cannot hurt the baby. Stop having sex if it hurts you. Stop having sex if there is blood on your panties or in the toilet.

Do we still need to use birth control?

No. But if you or your partner has an STD, you should use a condom.

Can the baby get sick if I get sick?

Not exactly. But alcohol, drugs, and medicine can hurt the baby. Do not drink alcohol or take any drugs or medicines if you are pregnant.

Is it normal to feel so tired?

Yes. Try to get more rest if you're tired all the time.

Why do I feel like crying all the time?

When a women is pregnant her body changes a lot. So do her feelings. It is normal to feel a little mixed up. Ask the people you live with to help. Ask them to understand. Soon you will feel better.

If I don't want the baby, can I cause a miscarriage?

No. Your feelings cannot hurt the baby. If you do not want a baby, tell your doctor or nurse. Talk about how you feel.

Things to Do in the First Trimester

1. Go to the doctor.
2. Eat good food.
3. Try to stop smoking.
4. Stay away from drugs and alcohol.
5. Start planning for your baby.

Chapter 4
The Middle Three Months

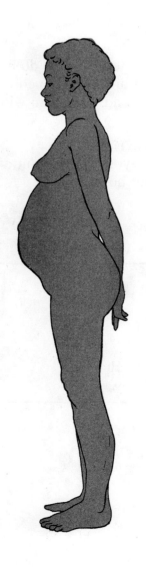

Months four, five, and six are the second trimester of pregnancy. The second trimester is like the middle of a good book. Many women say they feel great during the second trimester.

What is happening to me?

Your body

During the fourth, fifth, and sixth months of pregnancy you will feel good. If you were sick before, now you feel better. Now you start to "show."

Remember to eat good food every day. Choose food from each of the four basic food groups. (See chapter 1 for more on choosing good food.)

Some women have food cravings. You may want ice cream, candy bars, or chips. It is OK to have some treats. But watch out! If you have them every day, you will get fat!

Some women want to eat things that are not food. If you start to eat something that is not food, STOP. Call the doctor. Never eat dirt, laundry starch, or other things that are not food.

Your feelings

By the middle of pregnancy, you can feel the baby move inside you. The baby is "real" in a new way. Feeling the baby move makes some women dream about babies. Some dreams are funny. Some are scary. It is normal to have dreams about babies. Use this space to write down your dreams. If you don't remember a dream, write down your feelings about having a baby.

_____

_____

_____

What is happening to my baby?

From now until your baby is born, it is called a fetus. *Fetus* means "unborn." The fetus grows very fast. In the fourth month, it is six inches long. By the sixth month, it is 12 inches long! Soon it will weigh one pound.

By now your baby has tiny bones. It can open its eyes and hear the sound of your voice. All of the baby's parts are there.

The fetus moves a lot. Soon you will feel it. It will flutter. It will tickle. Sometimes it feels like butterflies in your tummy.

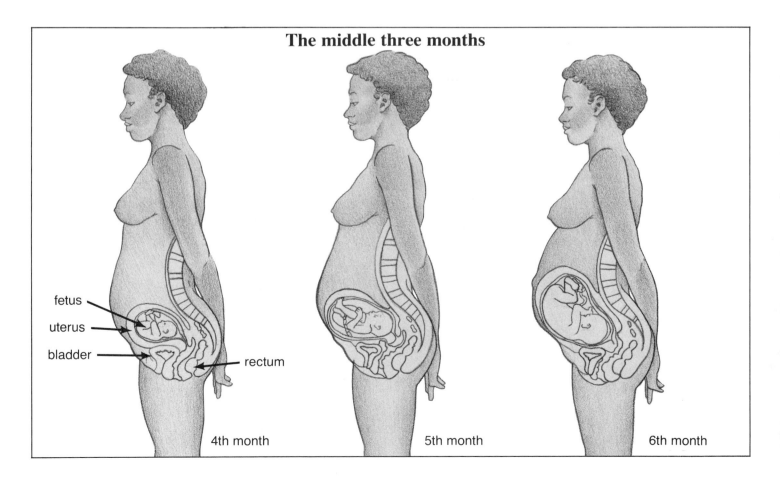

The middle three months

fetus
uterus
bladder
rectum

4th month   5th month   6th month

Some problems in the second trimester

Heartburn

Some women have heartburn after they eat. It feels horrible but it is not dangerous. Tell your doctor if you have heartburn.

Leg cramps

If you have a leg cramp, flex your foot. Push your heel out and bend your toes up to the ceiling.

Backache

If your back hurts, do not wear high heels. Do not lift very heavy things.

Here are some exercises for your back:

1. The pelvic rock
   Start on your hands and knees.
   Make your back flat.
   Round it up.
   Make it flat again.

2. Modified sit-ups
   Lie on your back, knees bent, feet flat on the floor.
   Lift your head up and reach to your knees.
   (If this makes you feel sick or dizzy, don't do it.)

Side pains

Side pains are normal. As your baby grows, your uterus and other muscles have to stretch. Sometimes this hurts.

Pins and needles

Sometimes women have a tingling feeling in their hands and fingers. It will usually go away after the baby is born.

Vaginal discharge

This is any liquid that comes out your vagina. It is normal to have a light discharge during pregnancy. Talk to your doctor if it is itchy, heavy, bloody, or has a bad smell.

Pelvic rock
    a. Start on your hands and knees, back flat.
    b. Round your back up.
    c. Make it flat again.

Modified sit-up
    a. Lie on your back, knees bent, feet flat on the floor.
    b. Lift your head up and reach to your knees.
    c. Lie flat again. Relax.

33

Kim talks:

When my baby moved, I thought I had a gas pain. But soon it felt like tickles and pokes. I loved it!

Cindy talks:

I felt great in the second trimester. I took long walks. I wore sneakers every day so my back did not hurt.

Maria talks:

I had trouble sleeping. I could not get comfortable. I put a pillow between my knees and one behind my back. It felt much better.

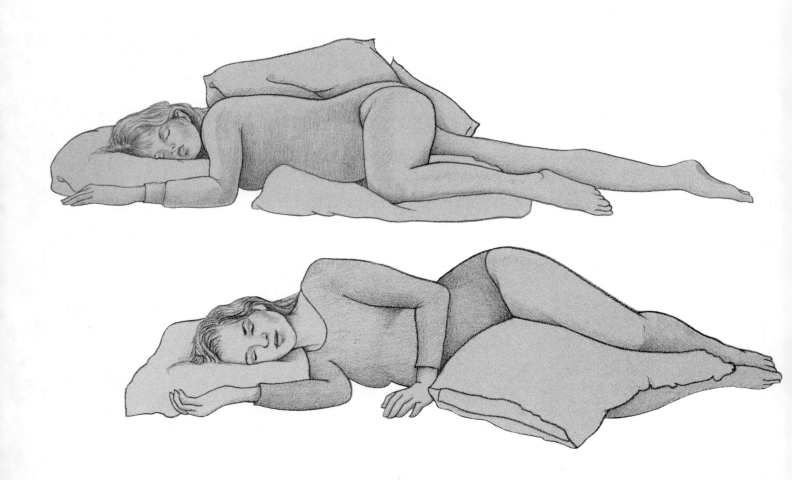

Questions and answers about the second trimester

Can I exercise now?

Yes! Go to a prenatal exercise class. Swim. Dance. Do not jump up and down. That might hurt your belly.

I have heard about a special exercise for my vagina. What is it?

It is called a kegel. (Some people call them Sheilas.) You should do them every day for the rest of your life!

Why?

Your vagina stretches during birth. Doing kegels helps keep the vagina in shape.

How do I do kegels?

You can do them any time, anywhere. Follow these steps:
1. Squeeze your vagina as if trying not to urinate.
2. Let go slowly.
3. Squeeze again. Let go slowly.

Do this exercise eight times. Do it every day.

Something white is leaking out of my nipples. What is it?

Your breasts are starting to make colostrum. This is your baby's first food. It tastes sweet. Just wipe it off.

I am getting stretch marks. What can I do?

Some women get stretch marks. Others do not. You can use creams, but they don't always help.

My skin itches. What can I do?

Use skin cream. But don't put it on your nipples.

I feel dizzy when I get up. How come?

Your body is making more blood to keep you and your baby healthy. If you move too fast, you will get dizzy. Move slowly. If you feel dizzy a lot, or if you faint, call your doctor.

Can I use a douche?

No.

I am constipated. What can I do?

Eat lots of fruits and vegetables. Try granola or bran cereal. Get some exercise. Drink plenty of liquids. Do not take any medicine unless your doctor gives it to you.

My bottom really hurts. Do you know why?

You may have hemorrhoids. Ask your doctor for a cream to help them.

Can I go on vacation?

Yes. You can travel in cars, trains, boats, or airplanes when you are pregnant. Be sure to wear your seat belt.

Does a woman lose a tooth every time she has a baby?

No. This is a superstition, or "old wives' tale." You do need to eat good food though, and take care of your teeth.

Old superstitions

Superstitions are often called "old wives' tales." They can cause a lot of worries. But most old wives' tales are not true.

Here are some old wives' tales about pregnancy. They are not true. Which ones have you heard? Have you heard others?

- Pregnant women should not go outside at night.
- If a mother gets scared or sees something bad, her baby will have a birthmark.
- If a pregnant woman scratches her belly, it will hurt the baby.
- If a pregnant woman reaches her arms up high, the baby will choke.

Things to Do in the Second Trimester

1. Go to the doctor.
2. Eat good food.
3. Find out about maternity leave from your job.
4. Find out where you will have the baby. Find out how much it will cost. Decide how you will pay for it.
5. Register for childbirth education classes.
6. Do you work? Will you go back to work? Look for a baby-sitter. Visit a day-care center that takes babies.

Chapter 5
The Last Three Months

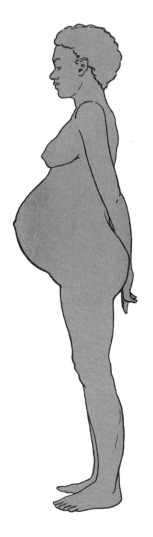

Word Guide		
bladder	sonogram	varicose veins
premature birth	ultrasound	

Months seven, eight, and nine are the last trimester of pregnancy. The third trimester is like the end of a good book. It is exciting. Soon you will have your baby.

What is happening to me?

Your body

In the third trimester, you will look and feel very pregnant. Your belly will be very big. You will move more slowly. You may feel very tired. Your back and feet may hurt. Try to rest whenever you can. Put your feet up. Don't wear high heels.

During the last trimester, you will feel the baby move. It will kick you hard. Sometimes it will tickle and make you laugh.

You will need to go to the bathroom a lot. This is because the baby is big and is pressing on your bladder.

Maria talks:

I had a backache. I think it was from lifting the other kids. I tried to rest, but it was hard.

Hal Silverman/Hal Silverman Studio

Your feelings

Some people say that a pregnant woman is very beautiful. You may feel beautiful. Or you may not. Some women feel very sexy when they are pregnant. They love to put lotion on their skin. They wear soft, baggy clothing. They feel very happy. They feel very special.

Some women do not feel so nice. They feel fat. They feel uncomfortable.

No matter how you feel, the best thing to do is relax. Soon the baby will come. Soon your body will feel normal again.

Sometimes women feel worried. You may worry about birth. You may wonder about how to take care of the baby. It's normal to worry. Tell your doctor or nurse how you are feeling. They will help you learn more about having a baby. They will help turn your worries into happy feelings.

> ### Cindy talks:
>
> *I didn't feel like going to school. But I went anyway. I really want to graduate from high school.*

> ### Kim talks:
>
> *I felt proud of the way my body looked.*

What is happening to my baby?

In the seventh, eighth, and ninth months, your baby grows bigger and stronger. You must still eat well. The baby needs a lot of food to keep growing and to get ready for birth.

Newborn babies usually weigh at least five pounds. Some babies weigh nine pounds or more. They have hair and fingernails. Some babies have a lot of hair.

When the baby is born, it will have a soft spot on its head. This is because the skull bones haven't grown together yet. The soft spot is normal. The bones grow together during the baby's first two years.

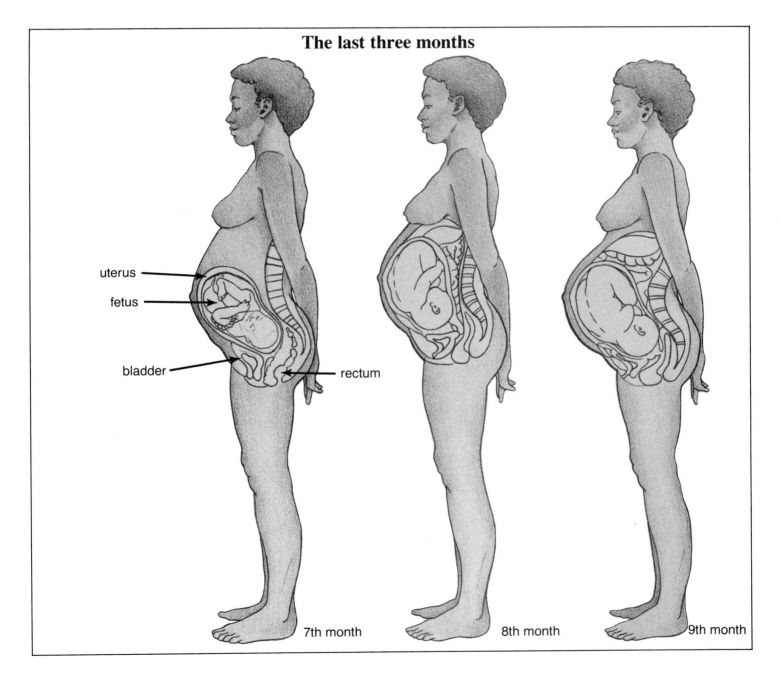

The last three months

uterus

fetus

bladder

rectum

7th month

8th month

9th month

Some problems in the last trimester

High blood pressure

Some women get high blood pressure when they are pregnant. It can be very dangerous. If your doctor tells you that you have high blood pressure, you should:

- Rest. Go to bed. Stay in bed if you can.
- Stay away from salty food.
- Try to relax. Listen to soft music.
- Take medicine IF the doctor tells you to.

Premature birth

Most babies stay inside their mothers for about nine months. Sometimes a baby is born too soon. A premature baby can be very sick.

If you feel like your baby is coming too soon, call your doctor. The doctor will want to see you right away.

Ways to prevent a premature birth:

- Eat good food.
- Drink plenty of water.
- Do not smoke cigarettes.
- Do not take drugs.
- Do not drink alcohol, wine, beer, or cocktails.
- Get off your feet when you can.

Warning signs in pregnancy
Call your doctor if you:

- have a bad pain in your belly
- have bleeding from your vagina
- cannot stop throwing up
- have a bad headache that will not go away
- have swollen hands or feet
- cannot feel the baby move
- have a fever
- have spots in front of your eyes
- have blurry vision
- can't go to the bathroom
- go to the bathroom more than usual
- have pain or burning when you urinate
- have water leaking out of your vagina
- have a bad cough

Questions and answers about the third trimester

My legs hurt all the time. I have big blue veins on my legs. What are they?

The big blue veins are called varicose veins. They can hurt. They happen because of the:

- weight of the baby
- hormones of pregnancy
- extra blood in your body

Things you can do:

- Wear support stockings.
- Sleep with your feet up on pillows.
- Rest with your feet up.

Some women have varicose veins around the vagina. They can hurt a lot. Try not to worry. They will go away after your baby is born.

Sometimes I get pains inside my vagina. Is this normal?

At the end of pregnancy you may feel pressure. Your vagina may ache. If you have a pain that does not go away, call your doctor.

When will my baby stop moving around?

Your baby should move inside you every day. It should not stop moving. Here are two things to do if you think your baby has stopped moving:

- Eat some food.
- Lie down.

After about half an hour, the baby should move. If the baby doesn't move, call your doctor.

Things to Do in the Last Trimester

1. Go to childbirth education classes. (See chapter 6.)
2. Arrange for maternity leave from your job.
3. Find a doctor for the baby.
4. Visit the hospital. Fill out pre-admission forms.
5. Decide how you will feed the baby. (More on this in chapter 10.)
6. Get things ready for the baby. (See next page.)
7. Pack your suitcase for the hospital. (See checklist below.)
8. Pack the things you'll need to bring your baby home in. (See checklist below.)

Pack these for the hospital:
- I.D., insurance card, health clinic card, welfare card
- robe, slippers, nightgown, toothbrush, toothpaste, comb
- make-up, shampoo, deodorant
- lollipops, hard candies, gum
- bra and panties, sanitary napkin belt
- comfortable clothes to go home in (not your best old jeans; they won't fit yet)
- about two dollars in change for phone calls
- a book or magazine

Do not take:
- jewelry
- a lot of money

Pack these to bring your baby home in:
- T-shirt
- nightgown
- two diapers, pins, and one pair of rubber pants

OR

- two newborn-size disposable diapers
- blanket

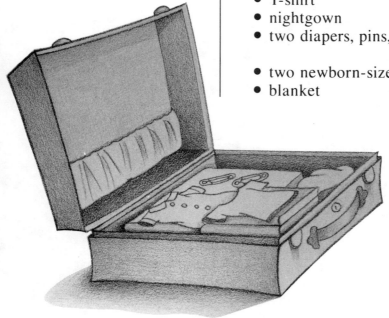

Baby will need these to start:
- three to six bottles (if you plan to use formula—more on this in chapter 10)
- three to four stretchy sleepers or nightgowns
- 24 diapers (more about diapers in chapter 10)
- two pairs of rubber pants
- two pairs of booties or socks
- six T-shirts
- two sweaters
- three to four soft baby blankets
- a safe place to sleep
- a car seat, if you have a car

Chapter 6
Learning about Birth

Hal Silverman/Hal Silverman Studio

Childbirth education

A long time ago, women learned about birth from their mothers. These days, many women go to childbirth education classes. This is not like school. You do not get grades.

In childbirth education class you learn how babies are born. You may see movies or videotapes of babies being born. You learn what will happen at the hospital. You learn what happens when your baby is born.

Ask your doctor or nurse about childbirth education classes. They will help you sign up for your class.

Hal Silverman/Hal Silverman Studio

In childbirth education classes, you and your helper learn what to expect. You learn how to relax, and how to get ready for birth.

Having a helper

Many women have a helper at birth. Your helper goes with you to your childbirth education classes. Your helper goes to the hospital with you. You should trust your helper.

Your helper can be the baby's father. Or it can be your mother, your sister, your aunt, or your best friend.

Who will be the best helper for you? _____

_____

Why will this person be a good helper for you? _____

_____

45

Cindy talks:

My mom came to class with me. She was my helper. At first I was sorry my boyfriend would not come. But my mom made me feel safe. It made us feel really close.

Maria talks:

I went to childbirth classes for my first baby. At first my husband didn't want to go. He said being with a woman during birth was no place for a man. I told him he put the baby in, now he had to help me get it out! In class he learned how to help me. I was glad he came with me.

In class

Childbirth classes help you know what to expect. You will learn about:

- how your body gets ready for birth
- labor and contractions
- medicine in the hospital
- giving birth

Getting ready for birth

Your body gives signs that your baby will soon be born. Here are four main signs. Not all women have all these signs.

1. **The baby "drops."**
   This is also called "lightening" or "engagement." It means that your baby is getting into the right position for birth.

2. **A "show" appears.**
   It is sometimes called a "bloody show." What "shows" is the mucus plug that had sealed the cervix. It's not very bloody; you may notice it on your toilet paper or in the toilet. Do not make love if you have a bloody show.

As your body gets ready for birth, the baby moves lower down, or "drops." Now you may find it easier to breathe. But you may have to go to the bathroom more often. The baby may press on your bladder.

It's good to lie down and rest when you can. At least sit down and put your feet up.

3. The bag of water breaks.

Sometimes the bag of water breaks before a woman goes into labor. It can happen during the day. It can happen at night. Water will come out your vagina. It can drip or it can gush. It will feel warm. The water should be clear or milky white.

Call your doctor if your water breaks. Tell the doctor if the water is brown or green or has a bad smell. If your water breaks, do not take a bath. Do not make love.

4. Contractions begin.

A contraction is a tightening of the muscles of the uterus. The uterus contracts, or gets tight.

The next section talks about contractions.

The baby "drops"

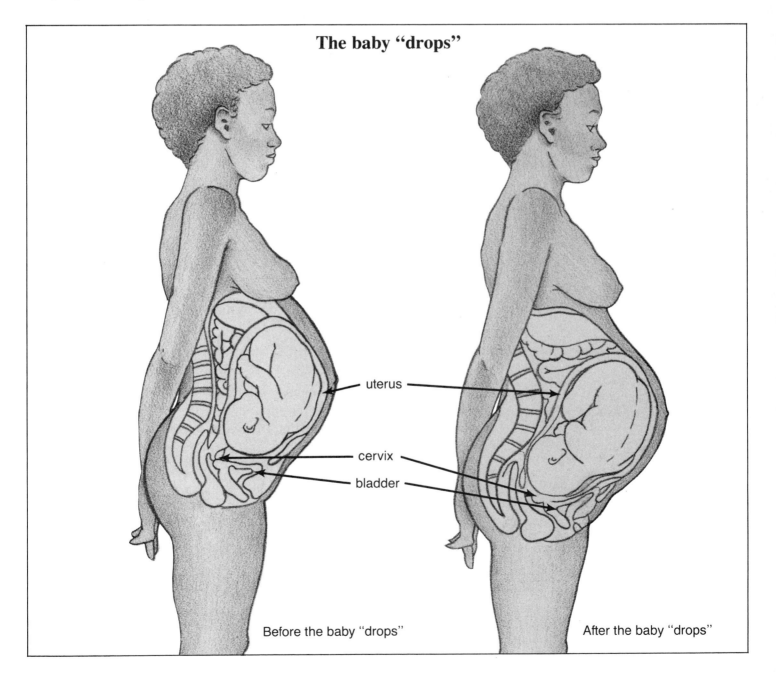

uterus

cervix

bladder

Before the baby "drops"

After the baby "drops"

Labor and contractions

Having a baby is called "being in labor." Labor is hard work. It can go fast (two to three hours), or it can take a long time (20-24 hours). First labors often last about 14 hours. But every labor is different.

When you are in labor, you have contractions. The muscles of the uterus contract—that is, they get shorter and harder. Then they relax. A contraction is like a wave. It starts small. It gets big. Then it goes away. You cannot make contractions start, or stop.

Normally, your cervix is shut tight, like a fist. Contractions open up your cervix. The cervix has to open, or dilate, so your baby can be born.

Sometimes contractions feel like bad cramps or a bad backache. You may feel them in your back. You may feel them across your belly. You may feel them down low inside your vagina.

No one knows how long her labor will be. Do you want to guess how long your labor will be? Write down your guess. After you have your baby, see how close you were.

I guess my labor will last ———————————— .

What to do when contractions start:

Call the doctor
Call your helper
Call the baby-sitter
Make sure your suitcase is packed
Watch TV, have a cup of tea, take a nap, take a walk

What not to do:

Do not eat a big meal
Do not clean up the house

Questions and answers about contractions

What do I do when I feel a contraction?
Take a deep breath and let the air out. Breathe in and out slowly. Tell your body to be soft. Tell your cervix to open.

Do contractions last a long time?
When they start, they are short—about 20-45 seconds long. They are 10-20 minutes apart. They don't hurt a lot. This is early labor.

After a while the contractions get longer—about 45-60 seconds. They are four to seven minutes apart. By now you will be in the hospital or on your way.

When the baby is almost ready to be born, the contractions come fast—they are about two minutes apart. They last about 90 seconds.

What is false labor?
False labor means contractions that do not open the cervix. Many women have false labor. Sometimes false labor can last for a long time. Here are two ways to tell if you have false labor:

1. If you have contractions during the day, sit down. Rest. If they go away, it is false labor.
2. If you have contractions at night, get up. Move around. If they go away, it is false labor.

Call the doctor if they don't go away.

Medicine in the hospital
In class you learn about medicine for labor and birth.

Medicine that helps you to relax is called a sedative. The nurse can give you an injection (shot) of a sedative.

You may also get it through an I.V. An I.V. is attached to your hand. The nurse puts a tiny, hollow needle in your hand. The medicine goes through a tube and through the needle.

Some medicine can take away feeling so you don't feel pain. This is called an anesthetic. There are many kinds of anesthetic. Two common ones used for childbirth are spinal and epidural.

If you get a spinal or an epidural, you will get an injection in your back. Then you won't feel any contractions. You won't feel anything in the lower part of your body.

Some women want to be "knocked out" for labor. This is not a good idea. Talk to your doctor about medicine.

Giving birth

Sometimes we hear scary stories about birth. We hear that it hurts.

It's true. Having a baby will hurt. It hurts because your cervix has to open. It has to open to let the baby out. But you don't have to be afraid. People will be there to help you. Birth happens all the time!

Natural childbirth

Many women do not want medicine for pain. They want natural childbirth. Natural childbirth means that you do not take any medicine.

If you want to try natural childbirth, tell your childbirth education teacher. She will teach you how to relax. She will teach you a special way to breathe. She will teach you what to do for the pain.

Cesarean birth

In class you will learn about cesarean birth. A cesarean is an operation. You will be given an anesthetic. The doctor cuts through your belly and uterus. The baby is lifted out. The operation takes about an hour. The doctor will decide if you need a cesarean.

Some reasons for having a cesarean are:
- The baby is sideways or feet down in the uterus (the head should come out first).
- The mother or the baby is very sick.
- The placenta is covering the cervix.

> ### *Kim talks:*
>
> *At first I was real scared about birth. In class they told us what to do if our water breaks or if we get a bloody show. They told us important things in every class. I went to every one. I learned so much. I wish everyone could go. Then women wouldn't be so scared.*

Maria talks:

I think the unknown makes you scared. When you are scared, then you feel the pain. I was scared for my first baby. With this baby, I don't feel scared.

Cindy talks:

They talked about cesareans in class. I did not think I would need one.

Then I had a sonogram. After the sonogram, my doctor said I might need a cesarean. She said the baby was lying sideways inside me.

I was scared. I called my teacher from the childbirth class. We talked on the phone. I asked her lots of questions. She didn't mind. She told me all about the operation. I felt a lot better after I talked to her.

Common positions of babies before birth

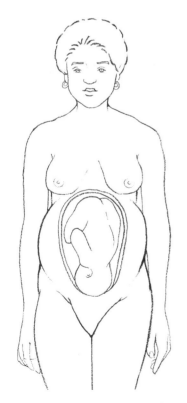

Normal position of the baby.

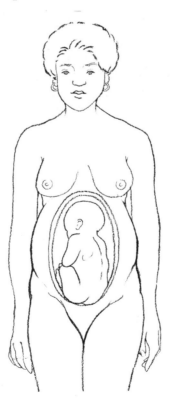

If the baby's feet come out first, it could harm the baby or the mother. A cesarean may be needed.

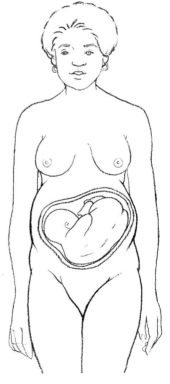

If the baby is sideways, the doctor may decide on a cesarean.

Chapter 7
Going to the Hospital

Word Guide

afterbirth	episiotomy	prep
enema	fetal monitor	vernex

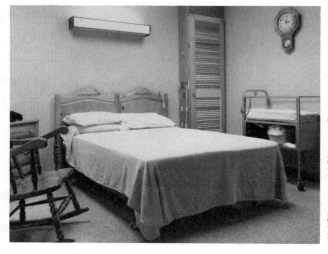

Hal Silverman/Hal Silverman Studio

Some hospitals have birthing rooms. They look more like a bedroom at home.

In America, most women have their babies in hospitals. Some women have their babies at birth centers. A birth center may or may not be part of a hospital. Others have their babies at home.

It is a good idea for you and your helper to visit your hospital or birth center before you have your baby. Find out where to go. Find out what door to go in. If you are going to drive to the hospital, find out where to park. You may be able to fill out the admission forms ahead of time.

Cindy talks:

I called a taxi when it was time to go to the hospital. What a ride! The driver was sure I would have the baby in the car!

When to go

Go to the hospital when your doctor tells you to, or when:
- contractions are five to seven minutes apart, or
- they last about 45 seconds, or
- your bag of water breaks, or
- you have blood coming from your vagina.

Don't forget to take your suitcase and insurance card or admission forms.

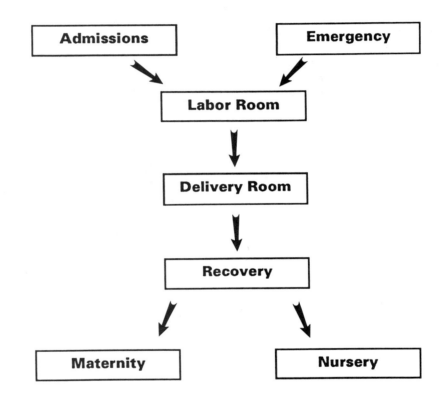

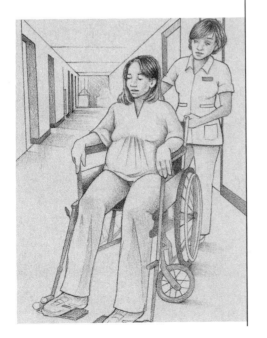

Where to go

You should know ahead of time exactly where to go first. It might be **Admissions**. It might even be **Emergency.** Your next stop will be **Labor and Delivery.** You may get to ride in a wheelchair. This is so you won't slip or fall.

You will go to a labor room. In the labor room there is a bed and a chair. You cannot eat in the labor room. Bring things to suck on. You can have a lollipop, gum, or hard candies.

You will get a hospital gown. It looks like a big shirt. It ties at the neck. It is open down the back. Remember to put on your robe if you go for a walk!

Labor

In the labor room the nurse will ask you how you feel. Tell her the truth. Tell her if you are afraid. Tell her if you feel sick. She will try to help you feel better.

The nurse will give you a pelvic exam. She will wear rubber gloves. She will check your cervix. Take a deep breath. Relax your body. It may hurt a little.

The nurse will check your blood pressure. She will take your temperature. She will listen to the baby's heartbeat.

The nurse may put a belt on your belly. This is called a fetal monitor. It will show the baby's heartbeat. It helps the nurse to see that your baby is OK.

The fetal monitor shows the baby's heartbeat. It may feel cold at first. It's a way of being sure that the baby is OK.

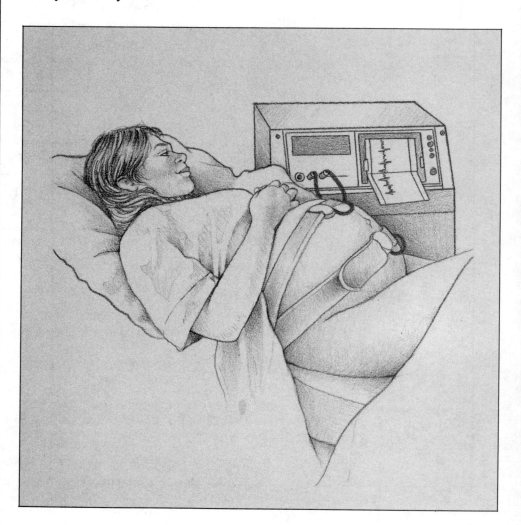

You don't have to lie down all the
time. You can sit up in a chair, or
walk around.

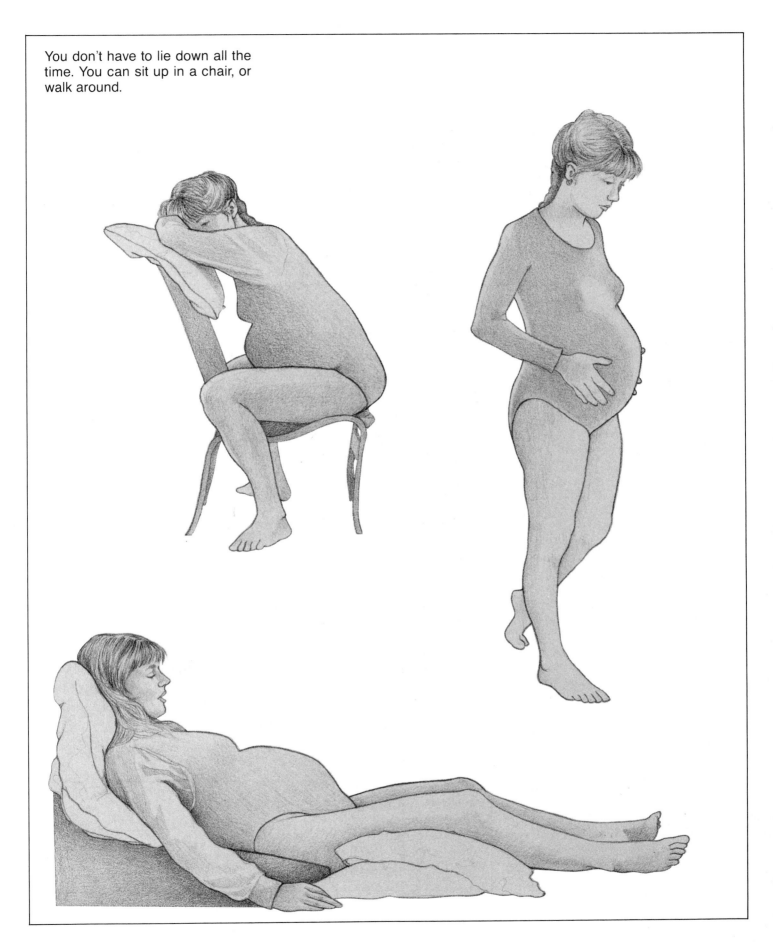

Questions and answers about labor

What is a prep?
"Prep" is short for "preparation." A nurse will get you ready for birth. She may shave the hair around your vagina. This is to keep the area clean. She may give you an enema. An enema cleans out your bowels. If you do not want a prep, tell your doctor before you go to the hospital.

How soon will the baby be born?
There is no way to know for sure. Some labors go fast. Some go slow. Some people say thinking good things helps a baby come faster.

What kinds of good things should I think about?
Think about your baby. Tell the baby you love him. Think about your vagina. Let it be soft and open. Let your body give birth.

What if my water breaks and I mess up the bed?
Don't worry. Disposable pads are on the bed. They can be changed if they get wet or messy.

Do I have to lie on my back in bed the whole time?
No. Do not lie on your back or stay in bed the whole time. Tell the nurse you would like to get up. You can sit up in bed or sit in a chair. You can walk around.

Can I go to the bathroom when I am in labor?
Yes. You should go every half hour.

What if I have a contraction in the bathroom?
Take a deep breath. Let the air out. Breathe slowly. Relax. The contraction will be over soon. Do not be afraid.

What if I have the baby in the bathroom?
Don't worry. Most babies don't come that fast. If it feels like the baby is going to be born, call your helper.

How does the baby know when to be born?
We do not know. Some people think that the baby decides when to be born. Some people think the placenta tells the baby. Some people think that the cervix tells the baby. Some people think that the uterus tells the baby. What do you think?

Kim talks:

My boyfriend drove me to the hospital. We were excited. When we got there he rubbed my back. He rubbed my legs. It felt great.

Delivery

Nurses and doctors will keep checking you. They want to know how your baby is doing. They look at the fetal monitor. They check your cervix to see how much it has opened.

When the cervix has opened enough, it's time for birth.

Your body works hard to give birth. Birth is exciting. It is special. You have made a new life. A new person will be born.

When it is time for birth, you may feel happy. You may feel tired. You may be afraid. Listen to the nurse. Listen to the doctor. They will tell you what to do. They will help you have a safe birth.

Contractions open up your cervix. The baby's head turns as it is pushed out. The outer skin stretches to let the baby through.

The birth process—from the outside

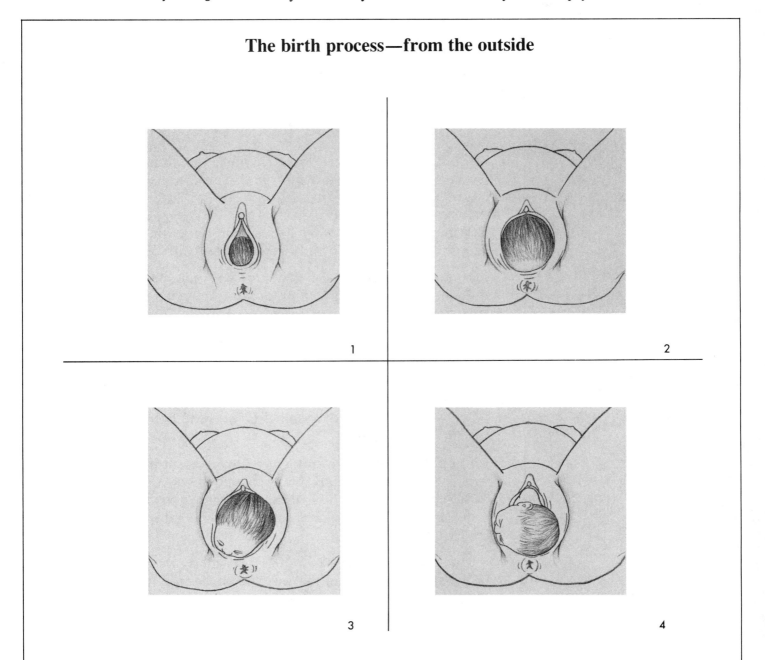

1

2

3

4

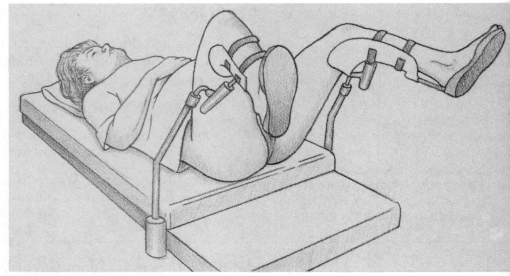

This is a common position for birth in a hospital. It's not the only one. You can sit, or kneel, or squat. You can lie on your side.

Positions for birth

There are many ways to have a baby. In some hospitals, you will go to a delivery room. In some hospitals, you can have the baby in a birthing room. A birthing room has a bed and feels a bit more like home.

You do not have to lie down on your back to have a baby. You can kneel. You can sit. You can squat. You can lie on your side.

Pushing the baby out

Pushing is more hard work. But your work is nearly over now. The nurse and doctor or midwife will help you.

When you push, your vagina stretches and opens up to let your baby out. When you push, think of your baby. It's ready to be born.

The doctor may make a small cut at the opening of your vagina. This is called an episiotomy. It makes the opening bigger. After the baby is born, the cut is stitched.

Your baby is born

At last, the moment has come! Is it a girl? Is it a boy? Now you know. The waiting is over.

You'll see your baby right away. Don't be surprised. Most newborn babies look funny. Some babies are covered with a white cream. The cream is called vernex. It protects the baby's skin inside the uterus. Some babies have dry skin. Some babies have puffy eyes, or oddly shaped heads.

You'll hear your baby cry. (They cry all by themselves—doctors don't need to spank them the way the stories tell it.) The doctor will clear out your baby's mouth and cut the umbilical cord. Your baby will get eyedrops, and a bracelet with its name on it.

You can hold your baby right away. You can breast-feed your baby if you want to.

The birth process—from the inside

With each contraction, the cervix opens more. When it is fully opened, the baby is born. This birth position is comfortable for many women.

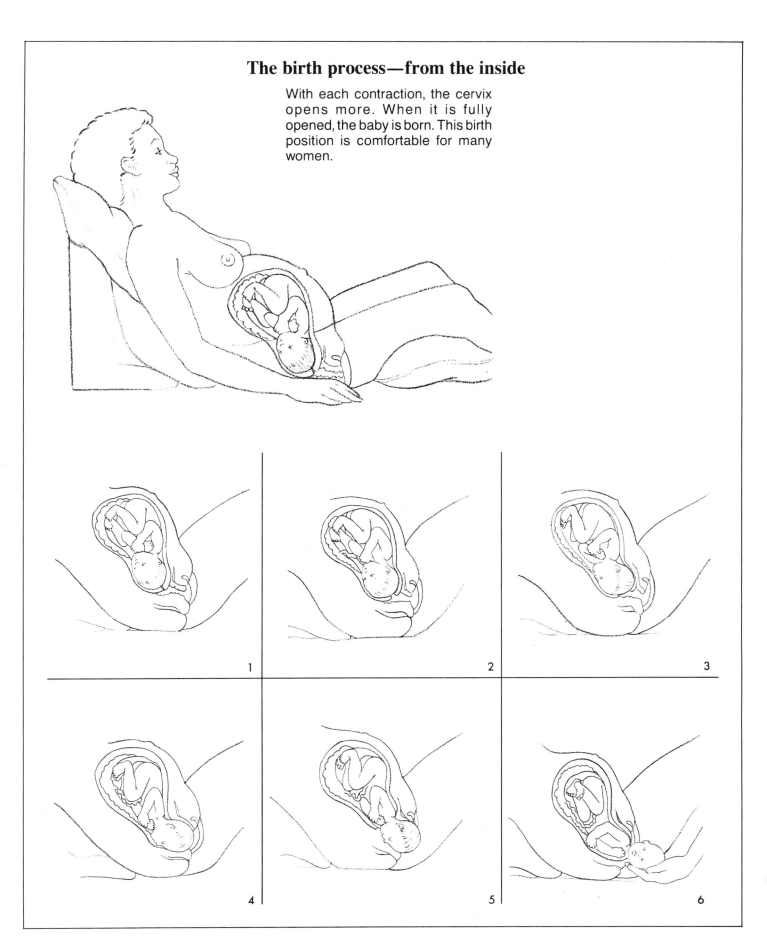

59

The afterbirth

One more thing happens. The placenta that fed your baby isn't needed anymore. The uterus pushes it out once the baby is born. That's why the placenta is often called the "afterbirth."

This takes a few minutes, or up to half an hour. When the placenta is out, labor is finished. Now your uterus will slowly shrink back to normal.

You will feel tired, sleepy, hungry, happy. Your legs may shake. You may want to cry. You are ready for the next move—to **Recovery.** Your baby will stay with you for a while, and then go to the **Nursery.**

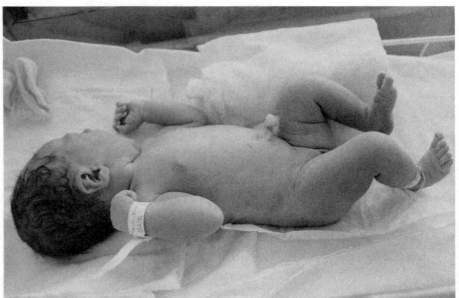

© 1989 Jeffrey High/Image Productions

Recovery

The nurse in Recovery will check you. She will push on your belly to check your uterus. Her push may hurt. Take a deep breath. Let the air out. Relax when she pushes.

The nurse will wash you up. She will have a pan with warm water. She will wash your bottom. Then you will go to **Maternity.**

You will stay in the hospital for one, two, or three days. You will rest and eat. When you get up, you may feel dizzy. Walk slowly. You can use the bathroom. You can take a shower.

In the hospital, you will start to get to know your baby. You will learn:
- how to feed your baby
- how to change your baby
- how to keep your baby clean

Questions and answers about birth

Do I have to have an episiotomy?

Not all doctors do episiotomies. Ask your doctor about it.

What do they do with the afterbirth?

First the doctor looks at it. The doctor makes sure that all the placenta is out. Then it is thrown out, along with the umbilical cord.

Why do they give the baby eyedrops?

The eyedrops protect the baby from eye infection and blindness. If a mother has an STD (sexually transmitted disease, V.D.), it can infect the baby. It can make the baby blind. The eyedrops prevent blindness. All babies get them.

Should I sit on pillows?

No. Sit on a hard chair.

Will my belly be flat right away?

No. It will take a few weeks to go down. When you start to exercise, your belly will get flatter.

Is it true that if you have a cesarean once, you will always have to have a cesarean?

No. You can talk to your doctor about having a VBAC (Vee-Back). VBAC means a "vaginal birth after cesarean."

What about the birth certificate?

Every baby has a birth certificate. Soon after your baby is born, you will fill out a birth certificate form. Your baby's full name will go on it. So will your name and the father's name. The baby's birth date will go on it, too. A few weeks later, you'll get the birth certificate in the mail. Check the names on it. Check the dates. Keep it safe.

Congratulations! You did a good job!

A special note:

If you have decided to give the baby up for adoption, you may or may not want to hold it. Some women do not even want to see the baby. It is up to you. Tell your doctor what you want.

Chapter 8
Three Births

Every birth is different. Some births are easy. Others are hard. The best thing a woman can do is not worry about birth. If you have taken care of your body, your mind, and your baby, you will be ready. Read what our three mothers have to say.

Maria talks first

My contractions started at night. I woke up. I felt my belly get hard. I took a deep breath. I let the air out slowly. I waited. Soon my belly got hard again. I knew the baby was on its way.

I got up. I went to the bathroom. I found my bloody show. It was pink. It was not very bloody.

I woke up my husband. I said, "Honey, we are going to have a baby soon."

He said, "Huh?" Then he jumped up. He started to run around. He grabbed his pants. He turned on the lights.

I started to laugh. "Not so fast," I said. "Go back to sleep. I will tell you when it's time to go to the hospital."

He laughed, too. We went back to bed. We couldn't sleep. We were too happy to sleep.

Soon the sun came up. I called my mother. She came to baby-sit.

I called the doctor. We went to the hospital.

My husband drove the car. We both wore our seatbelts.

In the hospital the nurse was nice. She checked me in. I had to sign some papers. She asked me about my contractions. I told her they were not too hard. I told her I wanted to have natural childbirth. I told her I didn't want any medicine.

I went into the labor room. The nurse gave me a hospital gown. She did an internal exam. My cervix was halfway open.

My husband came in. We played cards. We talked.

Soon my contractions got longer. They felt harder. I didn't want to play cards anymore. I had to close my eyes. I had to relax. We turned off the lights and closed the door. I tried to be relaxed.

The nurse knocked on the door. She came in and asked how I was. I told her I felt a little sick. I told her my back hurt.

She told my husband to rub my back. She put a hot towel on my back. That felt great.

My doctor came in. He checked my cervix. He said I was ready to go to the delivery room. I was glad!

When a contraction came, I took a deep breath. Then I pushed. The nurse said, "Look for the baby." When I pushed I looked for the baby.

The pushing was hard. I sat up. I rested on my side. The baby was coming slowly. I felt tired.

Finally I felt a sting. I felt my vagina open wide. I yelled, "Here comes the baby!" The baby came out. It was big and healthy. It started to cry.

"It's a boy," the nurse said.

"I love you," said my husband.

I was so happy. I cried.

The doctor let my husband cut the cord.

The thing I want to tell you is that having a baby is not that bad. Pushing the baby out can take a long time. But it is worth it!

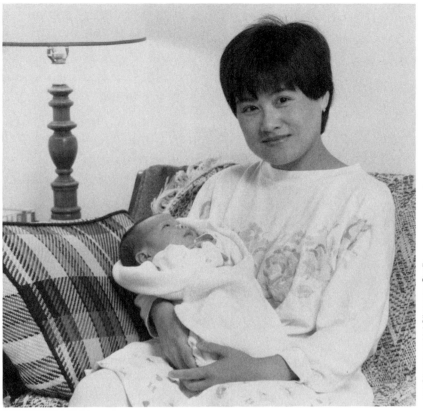

Kim talks

I went to work on Friday. I felt tired. My back hurt. At lunchtime I talked to my boss. She said to go home.

At home I took a nap. When I woke up my pants were wet. I knew my water broke. I went to the bathroom to check it. It was clear.

I called the clinic. They said it was time to go to the hospital. I called my boyfriend. He came over. I got my suitcase. Off we went!

The hospital was crowded. They didn't have a room for me. I sat in a chair. I was upset. My boyfriend told me it would be OK. He rubbed my back. I knew he felt bad, too.

Soon they had a room for me. The nurse put the fetal monitor on me. I could see that my baby was doing fine.

My contractions felt very hard. I asked for some medicine. My doctor came and checked me. She said I could have some medicine to help me relax.

My boyfriend asked her three questions: "What is the medicine? What does it do? What will it do to the baby?"

The doctor said the medicine was a sedative. She said it would help me to relax. She said it would not hurt the baby.

The nurse gave me an I.V. They put it in my hand. I got the medicine through the I.V. It made me sleepy.

Soon it was nighttime. My contractions were coming fast. They hurt a lot. I asked for more medicine. This time I got a spinal. It made me numb. I didn't feel the contractions at all. I liked that a lot.

The nurse checked me two times. Then she said I could start to push. I didn't feel anything. But I tried to push. She said I was doing a good job.

Then I went to the delivery room. Two nurses helped me. They put my legs in the stirrups. I was happy. I didn't feel any pain.

The doctor came in. She said to push. I pushed but I didn't really feel it.

She gave me an episiotomy. I didn't feel it.

The baby came out slowly. It had a lot of hair. It was a girl!

The doctor cut the cord.

Then she told me to push again. The afterbirth came out. The doctor said it looked fine. Then she sewed up the episiotomy.

My boyfriend was happy. I felt great. I was so happy to see my baby!

Hal Silverman/Hal Silverman Studio

Cindy talks

I knew I needed a cesarean. The doctor told me that my baby was big and healthy. But she said the baby was lying sideways inside me. I wanted to know when she would do the operation. She told me she didn't know when. She said I should go into labor. She said it was good to feel some contractions.

On Sunday night I felt contractions. They didn't hurt. But they did not go away. I called my doctor. She wasn't there. Another doctor called me back. He said to come to the hospital.

My mother helped me a lot. I was shaking. She put a cool washcloth on my forehead. I felt better.

In the hospital I had to sign some papers. Then I had another ultrasound. It showed the baby was still sideways.

A nurse came into my room. She shaved my belly. She told me what would happen next.

In the delivery room, they gave me an anesthetic for pain. After the shot I did not feel my body. I did not feel my legs. Then they put straps on my arms.

The doctor made a cut through my belly. Then he made a cut in my uterus. I didn't feel it. I talked to the doctor. I talked to my mother. We guessed the baby was a girl.

The doctor lifted my baby out. I had a new baby boy! I was surprised. I was happy. My mother kissed me. We all cried.

I stayed in the hospital for one week. My belly hurt. They gave me some medicine for the pain. The cesarean was not so bad.

Chapter 9

Going Home

Word Guide	
lochia	postnatal

You will stay in the hospital for just a few days. Then it will be time to go home.

Now you are a mother. Now you have three important things to do:
Take care of your body.
Take care of your mind.
Take care of your baby!

Take care of your body

Pregnancy changed your body. Giving birth changed your body more. Now that you are a mother your body is changing again. You may like some of the changes. You may not like others.

Now is the time to be good to yourself. Now is the time to be proud of yourself. Feel good about yourself as you learn to be a mother.

How has your body changed since you had the baby? _____

_____

How do you feel about the changes? _____

_____

What can you do about them? _____

_____

You will go back to your doctor or clinic when the baby is six weeks old. This is called your six-week postnatal checkup. *Postnatal* means "after the birth." Tell the doctor how you feel.

You can bring the baby. The people who took care of you will be happy to see the baby.

Things to know about

An episiotomy (if you had one):
The episiotomy cut through the skin and muscle around your vagina. If you had an episiotomy, keep your bottom clean. Do your kegel exercises. Call the doctor if your episiotomy hurts.

A cesarean (if you had one):
You will stay in the hospital about a week. Your belly will hurt when you move. When you go home, do not go up and down stairs. Ask someone to help you with the baby. Call your doctor if the cut gets very sore, red, or starts to hurt more.

The lochia:
After birth you will have a discharge from your vagina. It is called the lochia. It is like having a light period. In the hospital, you wore sanitary napkins. Keep wearing them at home. Do not wear tampons. The lochia will turn brown and stop in three or four weeks. Call your doctor if it gets red and heavy.

After pains:
After the baby is born, your uterus is very big. It has to get small again. It contracts. If you feel the uterus contracting, you are feeling after pains. Take a deep breath and relax. The pains go away in about three days.

Food for you:
Good food is still important. Choose from the four basic food groups. Eat fresh food. Good food is always important for your health.

Losing weight:
Most mothers want to lose weight fast. But be patient. It takes nine months to make a baby. It can take nine months to lose all that weight. Do not worry. Your body will feel and look better soon.

Getting back into shape:
Start exercise slowly. Go for a walk. Turn on some music and dance! Some mothers go to exercise classes.

Getting back in shape

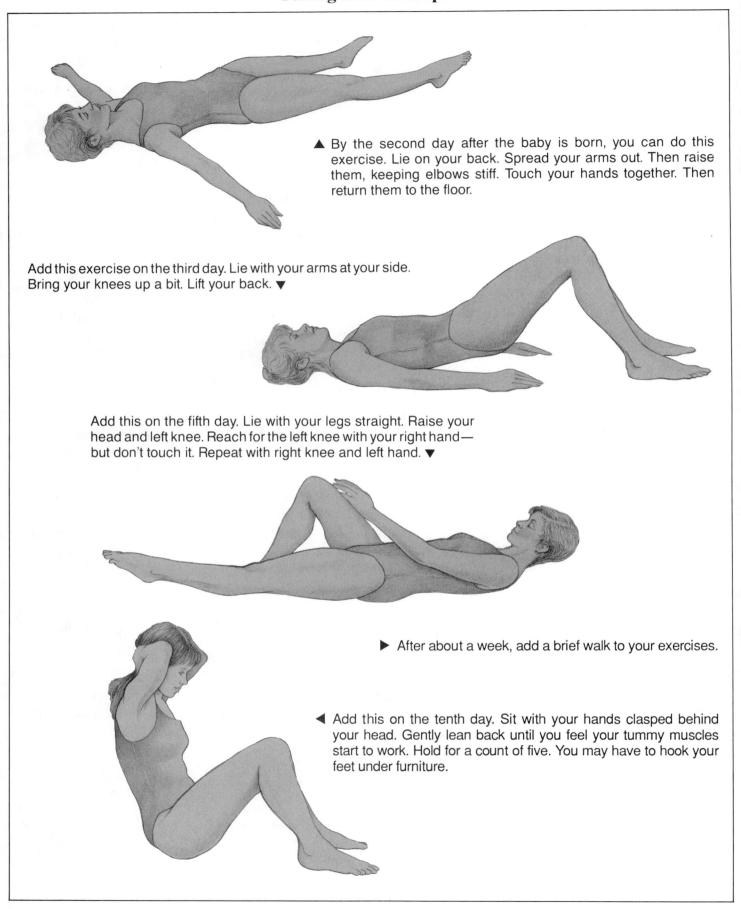

▲ By the second day after the baby is born, you can do this exercise. Lie on your back. Spread your arms out. Then raise them, keeping elbows stiff. Touch your hands together. Then return them to the floor.

Add this exercise on the third day. Lie with your arms at your side. Bring your knees up a bit. Lift your back. ▼

Add this on the fifth day. Lie with your legs straight. Raise your head and left knee. Reach for the left knee with your right hand— but don't touch it. Repeat with right knee and left hand. ▼

▶ After about a week, add a brief walk to your exercises.

◀ Add this on the tenth day. Sit with your hands clasped behind your head. Gently lean back until you feel your tummy muscles start to work. Hold for a count of five. You may have to hook your feet under furniture.

> ### Cindy talks:
>
> *When I came home, I slept on the couch. I kept the baby next to me. It hurt me to move. But I got better fast.*

> ### Kim talks:
>
> *I love to exercise. I took long walks. It was fun to be out with my new baby.*

Breast care:
If you are breast-feeding, keep your breasts clean. Wash them with water. Call your doctor if:
- your nipples crack or bleed
- your breast is red
- your breast is hot and sore

(There is more on breast-feeding in the next chapter.)

Going to the bathroom:
If your urine is dark or has a strong odor, drink more water. Drink eight glasses of water each day. Call your doctor if:
- you feel that you have to go to the bathroom but nothing comes out
- it hurts or burns when you urinate
- you pass any blood when you urinate

Making love:
Your doctor will probably tell you to wait six weeks. After that, sex is fine:
- when you feel you are ready
- when the lochia stops
- as long as it does not hurt

Do not make love if you don't want to. If you don't want another baby right away, remember to use birth control. Ask your doctor what kind of birth control you should use. If you use the pill, you cannot breast-feed your baby. (See pages 94-96 for birth control information.)

> ### Maria talks:
>
> *After we came home I was tired. I didn't feel sexy. My husband felt bad. It took me a long time to want sex. We waited about six weeks. When we made love he was gentle, but it hurt me. We waited another few weeks. Now things are back to normal. I feel much better.*

Take care of your mind

Having a new baby can make you feel very happy. Sometimes it can make you feel very sad. Sometimes women get the "baby blues." After the baby is born, they feel sad.

Babies are a lot of work. After you have a baby, your whole life seems to change.

Here are some things to do if you have the blues:
- Get some extra rest. Nap when the baby is asleep.
- Get some help with the housework. Ask everyone to help out.
- Go on a picnic. Go to the zoo.
- Get back into shape.
- Talk to someone who cares.

Some moms need to talk about birth. It helps them to feel better.

> ### Kim talks:
>
> *My friends all wanted to know about the birth. I told them everything. I felt very proud.*

> ### Cindy talks:
>
> *I didn't want to talk about the birth. I didn't feel bad or sad. I just didn't feel like talking. My mother said that was OK.*

Talking about birth

Write about having your baby. Share your story and your feelings if you want to.

How did you feel in the hospital?

What do you remember about your labor?

Did you have medicine?

How did the medicine make you feel?

Who was your helper?

Who was your doctor?

Who was your nurse?

Do you remember what you said when the baby was born?

_____

_____

_____

_____

_____

_____

_____

_____

_____

_____

_____

_____

_____

_____

_____

_____

_____

_____

_____

Take care of your baby

Let's start by getting to know your baby

Is it a boy or a girl? _____

The baby's name is _____

The baby is named after _____

The baby's birthday is _____

At birth, the baby weighed _____

What time was it born? _____

Does it sleep a lot? _____

Does it cry a lot? _____

You can put a picture of your baby here

What it's like to be a baby

When the baby is newborn . . .

A newborn baby can look at her mommy's face. She can suck on a bottle, a breast, or on her own hands. She can cry. She can sleep.

She can hear, taste, feel, touch, see, spit up, burp, and blink. She can move her head a little. She can move her hands, arms, and legs.

A newborn baby needs you to hold her. She cannot sit up. She cannot hold up her head. She cannot roll over.

She will sleep for two or three hours at a time. Then she will wake up to eat. She will wake up to eat during the day and at night.

A newborn baby can make tiny noises. She can look at pictures and faces. She will get scared if you put her down too hard or play too rough.

When the baby is two months old . . .

When your baby is two months old, he will smile at you. He still needs you to hold him. He loves to be close to you. He will know your voice. He will feel safe with you.

He will still wake up to eat at night. When he wakes up you should feed him, change him, and put him back to bed. If you play with him at night, he will not go back to sleep.

He still cannot sit up or crawl or hold his toys.

When the baby is three months old . . .

When your baby is three months old, she will sleep better at night. She will be awake more during the day.

She loves her bath. She will splash the water.

She loves to suck. She loves to eat. She grows best on breast milk or her bottle. She does not need any other food yet.

Play with your baby

Your baby will like to play with you. He will look at you. He will look at his toys. Keep his toys clean. Never give him toys that look like this:

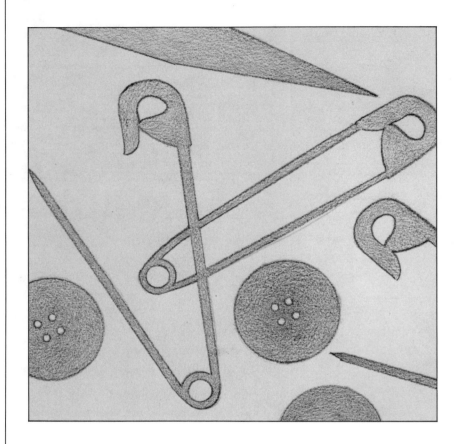

You can help your baby learn. Play with your baby. Here are some ideas:

- Hold your baby and dance.
- Play soft music for your baby. Sing to him.
- Talk to your baby. Tell him his name.
- Kiss his nose. Count his toes.

Can you think of other ways to play with your new baby?

_____

_____

_____

_____

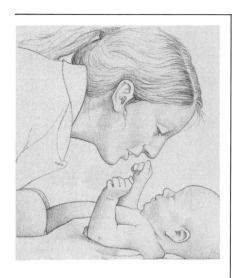

Be gentle with your baby

All babies need love. They need to feel warm and safe. If you feel mad at your baby remember that she is tiny. Always be gentle. Never hit her. Never shake her.

Here are some things you can do if you get mad:
- Take a deep breath and count to 10.
- Put the baby in his crib. Never throw the baby into his crib.
- Sit down and relax.
- Call your mother, the baby's dad, or a friend.
- Listen to music.
- Put the baby in a backpack or carriage. Go out for a walk. (Make sure you dress the baby in the right kind of clothes. If it is hot, do not put on too many blankets. If it is cold outside, make sure he is warm.)

All new mothers have questions about how to take care of their babies. In the next chapter, we will talk about taking care of your baby.

Draw yourself a rainbow here. A rainbow means good luck.

Chapter 10
Baby Care

Word Guide

circumcision	diarrhea	labia
constipation	disposables	pediatrician
convulsion	formula	

Being a mother means making good decisions. You will learn different ways to take care of a baby. You will decide how you will take care of your baby.

At first, it may seem hard. Just remember that your baby needs you. Your baby needs your love. Love your baby. Take good care of your baby. It is the most important job of your life.

The first thing to decide is how to feed your baby.

Feeding baby: bottle or breast?

A new baby eats every two or three hours. You will feed your new baby eight to 12 times a day. The baby needs breast milk or formula.

Hal Silverman/Hal Silverman Studio

Bottle-feeding

Why use formula?
- If you use formula, someone else can help feed the baby. You don't always have to be there.
- You can smoke or drink if you want to.

Why not use formula?
- You have to buy formula. It is expensive. You must always have some on hand. If you run out, the baby will have nothing to eat.
- Bottles must be kept very clean. Dirty bottles can make a baby very sick.
- You have to have a bottle with you all the time.

If you decide to use formula, you will need:
- three to six bottles
- three to six nipples
- three to six nipple caps
- one bottle brush for washing
- cans of formula. Ask your nurse how much to buy. Ask her what kind to buy. Write it down.

Formula comes three ways: ready-to-use, powdered, and concentrated. If you buy ready-to-use formula, follow the directions on the label. If you buy powdered or concentrated formula, you will have to add water. Follow the directions on the label.

If you use formula, remember this word: CLEAN. The water must be clean. The bottles must be clean.

Do not add sugar, honey, or molasses to the baby's formula. Do not make the baby finish the bottle if he doesn't want it. Give the baby more if he seems hungry. You can keep bottles of formula in the refrigerator for two days.

Breast-feeding

Why breast-feed?
- Breast milk is the best food for babies.
- You don't have to buy it. It is always ready. You will not run out of breast milk.
- You can be close to your baby. Even if you are very busy, you can breast-feed.

Why not breast-feed?
- You may feel messy.
- You can't smoke or drink if you're breast-feeding.

Tips for breast-feeding your baby:
- Take a deep breath and relax.
- Hold the baby so it faces your breast.
- Make sure the baby sucks on your nipple and the dark skin around it.

After five to 10 minutes, you'll want to move the baby to your other breast. Don't pull the baby off your nipple—it will hurt. Open the baby's mouth gently with your finger. Now:
- Burp the baby.
- Let the baby suck on your other breast for five to 10 minutes.

Questions and answers about feeding the baby

If I breast-feed do I have to drink a lot of milk? I hate milk.
You don't have to drink milk. Drink juice or water. Do not drink coffee or cola. The caffeine in them is not good for the baby.

Can medicine get into my milk?
Yes. Do not take any drugs or medicine unless your doctor tells you to.

When I nurse, how long should my baby suck?
Most babies like to suck. In the beginning, let her suck for about 10 minutes on each side. After you get used to it, let the baby suck longer.

How will I know when to feed the baby?
Your new baby will sleep a lot. When he wakes up he will cry. Feed him when he cries. He may wake up every two hours. He may wake up every three or four hours.

Will I make enough milk?
Most mothers make plenty of milk. You should eat lots of good food. Drink plenty of water, juice, milk, or soup. The more often you breast-feed, the more milk you will make.

How do I know if the baby is getting enough food?
The baby should wet her diaper six to 10 times a day. Wet or dirty diapers mean the baby is getting enough milk.

I want to bottle-feed my baby. Where do I buy formula?
You can buy formula at the food store. You can buy it at the drugstore. Check the prices. You can use food stamps.

How often do babies mess their diapers?
If you are breast-feeding, your baby may have a bowel movement after almost every feeding. The bowel movement will be yellow and soft. If you are bottle-feeding, your baby should have a bowel movement at least one or two times a day. It will be brown.

The baby's bed

Where will your new baby sleep? In a cradle? In a crib? Very tiny babies can sleep in a carriage. A baby can sleep in a big, clean, open box.

Will the baby sleep in your room? Will the baby have her own room? The baby's room should be clean. It should not be too hot or too cold.

Your baby will sleep a lot. Make sure her bed is safe. Be sure you can hear the baby when she cries.

Things to know about the baby's bed:
- Change the sheets whenever the baby's bed is wet.
- Keep the crib clean. Wash it. Make sure there are no bugs in it.
- Keep the mattress clean. It should not smell bad.

Hal Silverman/Hal Silverman Studio

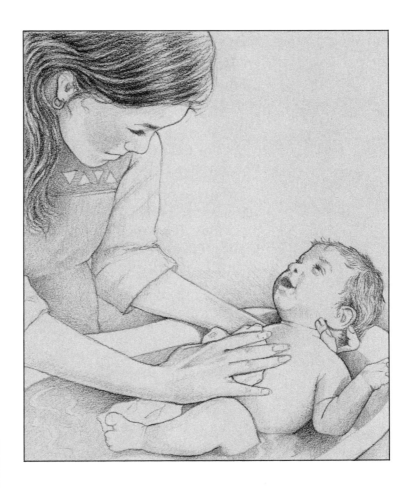

The baby's bath

Remember: Safety first!

At first you will give the baby a sponge bath. You won't put the baby in water. Have a small pan nearby with warm water in it. Use a soft cloth to wash the baby. Wash the baby every day.

When the baby's navel (belly button) has healed, you can give the baby a bath.

Things to know about the baby's bath:
- Put a towel in the sink. This will make the sink feel soft.
- Put two or three inches of warm water in the sink. Do not make it too deep. It should not be too hot. It should not be too cold.
- Wash the baby's face first.
- Do not use soap or shampoo. Use plain, warm water.
- Use a soft cloth or cotton balls to wash the baby.
- NEVER leave your baby alone in the bath. If the phone rings or someone is at the door, TAKE THE BABY WITH YOU.

The baby's diapers

Babies use lots of diapers. Diapers are a big part of a new mother's life. Change your baby's diaper as soon as it is wet or soiled. Wipe the baby's bottom from front to back. Make sure the baby's bottom is clean and dry.

What kind of diapers should you use? It's another decision you'll have to make. There are cloth diapers and disposable diapers.

You can buy cloth diapers or use a diaper service. Diaper services are especially helpful for mothers who don't have washing machines. They pick up soiled diapers and deliver clean ones. Figure out what the local diaper service charges per diaper. Compare the cost to the cost of disposables. See which is better.

Here are some reasons people give for and against different kinds of diapers.

Cloth diapers

Why use cloth diapers?
- You buy them once. They don't cost a lot of money.
- They are soft.
- You can fold them to fit any size baby.

Why not use cloth diapers?
- You have to wash them.
- Some people think they are old-fashioned.

Disposable diapers

Why use disposables?
- They are easy to use.
- You don't have to wash them.

Why not use disposables?
- Some babies get rashes from them.
- They cost a lot of money—even a diaper service often costs less.
- They are a big part of the nation's trash problem.

Why is my baby crying?

All babies cry. Some babies cry a lot. Sometimes it is hard to know why a baby is crying.

Here are some things to do if your baby is crying:
- Check his diaper. Change it if it's wet or soiled.
- Feed the baby. Burp the baby.
- Sing to the baby. Rock him. Carry him around with you.
- Is the baby too hot or cold? You can change his clothes.
- Do you think the baby is sick? Call the doctor if you think the baby is sick.

If your baby is clean and dry and does not want food, he may just be tired. Put him to bed. He may cry for five or 10 minutes and then go to sleep. If your baby's crying makes you angry or upset, **STOP.** Don't hit or shake him. Don't yell at him. Talk about your feelings with others.

If you have no one to talk to, find out if your city has a telephone hotline. Keep the number handy. Hotlines offer help.

Hal Silverman/Hal Silverman Studio

How to take care of . . .

The umbilical cord
Keep it dry and clean. The scab will fall off in a week or two. Call the doctor if it gets very sore, starts to bleed, or smells bad.

Circumcision
If you had your baby boy circumcised, the skin on the head of the penis will be red and tender. Cover it with vaseline. Keep it dry and clean. It will be healed in four or five days.

If you did not have your baby boy circumcised, you must keep the penis clean. Be gentle. Do not pull on the skin.

The labia (a baby girl's bottom)
Baby girls need to be dry and clean. Sometimes they have a tiny discharge from the vagina. Call the doctor if it is heavy or smells bad.

Diaper rash
Diaper rash can hurt. Change the baby's diapers when they are wet or soiled. Ask your doctor about a cream for the baby's bottom.

Diarrhea
Your baby has diarrhea if she has loose, runny bowel movements many times a day. Diarrhea can make your baby very sick. Give her a bottle of cool water. (Boil the water first to make sure it is clean.) Do not give her juice. Call your doctor if you think your baby has diarrhea.

Constipation
Your baby is constipated if he has trouble making a bowel movement, and the bowel movement is hard and dry. Give the baby cool water. Boil the water first to make sure it is clean. Call your doctor if your baby is constipated.

Dry skin
Wash with water only. Do not use soap. Ask your doctor about using a cream.

Cradle cap
This is dry skin on the baby's head. Wash the baby's head very gently. Do not use oil, unless your doctor suggests one.

Spitting up
Most babies will spit up a little bit when they burp. Call the doctor if your baby spits up hard after every feeding.

Thrush
Thrush is an infection. You will see white spots inside the baby's mouth or on his lips. They don't come off if you wipe them. Call the doctor if you think your baby has thrush.

Colic

Some babies get bad bellyaches. They cry a lot, usually in the evening. Try to help the baby. Walk her. Pat her. Talk softly to her. Sing to her. Do not get mad at the baby. Colic usually goes away after three months.

Checkups for the baby

Regular checkups are important. Take your baby to the pediatrician or to the clinic when he is two weeks old.

The doctor will check the baby. Tell the doctor if the baby has any problems. The doctor will help you. Never give the baby any medicine unless the doctor tells you to.

If you have any questions about baby care, you can ask the doctor.

When the baby is six weeks old he will start getting shots to protect him from disease.

Here is a list of the shots the baby will get. The baby must get all of these shots. DPT stands for diphtheria, pertussis, tetanus. (Pertussis is whooping cough.) MMR stands for measles, mumps, and rubella. (Rubella is German measles.) You must bring the baby to the doctor for the shots. Write down the date the shot is given to the baby.

Shots your baby needs

Polio (given by mouth)	When it is given:	Date given to your baby:
first dose	6-12 weeks of age	_____
second dose	8 weeks later	_____
third dose	8 weeks later	_____
first booster	1 year later	_____
second booster	3 years later	_____
DPT		
first dose	6-12 weeks of age	_____
second dose	4-6 weeks later	_____
third dose	4-6 weeks later	_____
first booster	1 year later	_____
second booster	3 years later	_____
MMR		
one shot	1 year of age	_____

When to call your baby's doctor

Call your baby's doctor or the clinic if:
- the baby is crying a lot and will not stop
- the baby seems too sleepy
- the baby will not eat
- the baby's bowel movement has blood or pus in it
- the baby seems hot or has a fever
- the baby has a rash
- the baby is in pain
- the baby has a convulsion: if she twitches, if her eyes roll back, if she cannot move
- the baby cannot breathe, or turns blue
- you drop the baby or if the baby falls

What to say when you call the doctor

Hello. I am calling for Doctor _____(your doctor's name)_____ .

My name is _____(your name)_____ .

My baby __(your baby's name)__ is ___(how old)___ .

He/She is _____(describe the problem)_____ .

Sometimes you need help fast. Keep a list of emergency numbers. If you need help fast:
- call the right number
- tell them who you are
- tell them what is wrong
- tell them where you live

Emergency phone numbers

Clinic _____

My doctor _____

Baby's doctor _____

Ambulance _____

Police _____

Fire _____

Poison Control _____

Neighbor _____

Friend with a car _____

Taxi _____

Some last thoughts

Some babies are born sick. They need special care. If your baby is born sick, you may feel scared. But you can learn how to take care of your baby. The nurses will help you learn.

Sometimes a baby dies. When a baby dies, everyone feels sad. If your baby dies, it is not because you were bad. You may have a lot of mixed-up feelings if your baby is sick or dies. You will feel better if you talk about how you feel.

Being a mother means learning to make good decisions. You cannot know everything right away. As your baby grows you will learn more. Just be sure to love your baby. Your love will light the way to a happy, healthy life.

Appendix

How Did This Happen?

How do you get pregnant? It's good to know. It's good to understand how your body works.

Look at the drawing of a woman's sex organs.

A woman's sex organs

The uterus is a strong muscle. It is hollow, and about the size of a fist. When you get pregnant, your baby grows inside your uterus.

The opening to the uterus is called the cervix.

On each side of the uterus is a tube. These two tubes are called the fallopian tubes. Each tube leads to an ovary. The ovaries are about the size and shape of almonds.

The ovaries have thousands of eggs in them. The eggs are already there when you are born. But they are not developed. They develop at the time you start having periods. This time is called puberty.

From this time on, an egg pops out of one of your ovaries each month. From this time on, you can get pregnant. The egg travels down the fallopian tube to the uterus.

Every month, the uterus gets ready to be a place for a baby to grow in. It stores extra blood and makes a thick, soft lining. If you don't get pregnant, the egg and the extra blood and lining in your uterus come out through the cervix. This is called menstruation or having your period.

Female sex organs

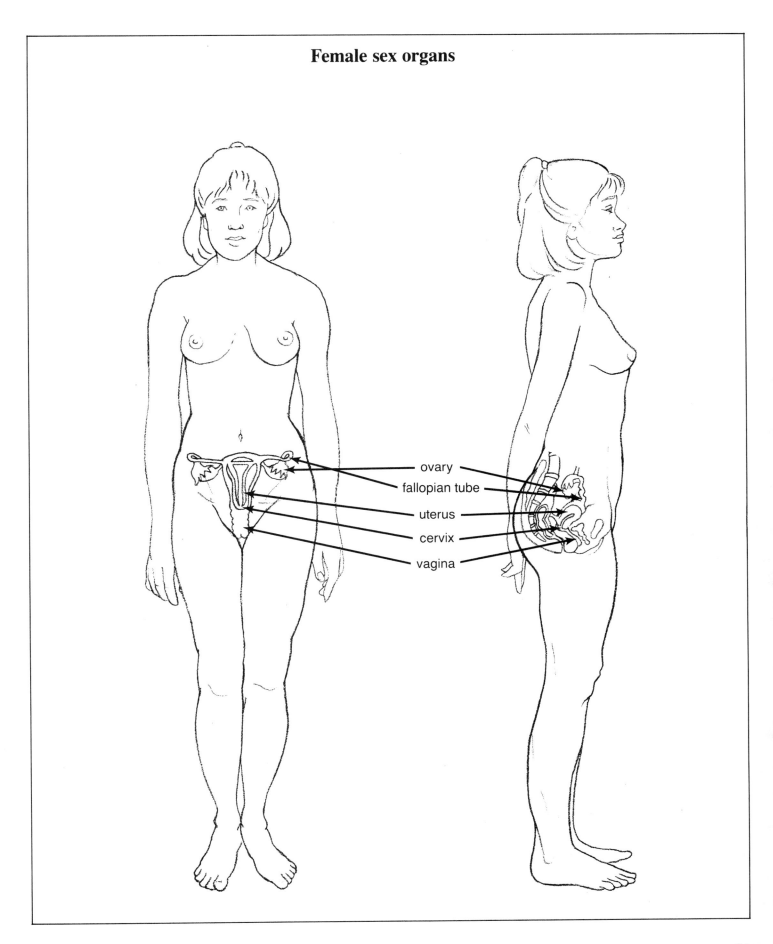

ovary

fallopian tube

uterus

cervix

vagina

A man's sex organs

Now look at the sex organs of a man. A man has two testes. The testes are in a bag of skin just behind the penis.

The testes make sperm, which are tiny cells. There are millions of tiny sperm. They are in a liquid called semen. The sperm travel through a tube from the testes to the penis.

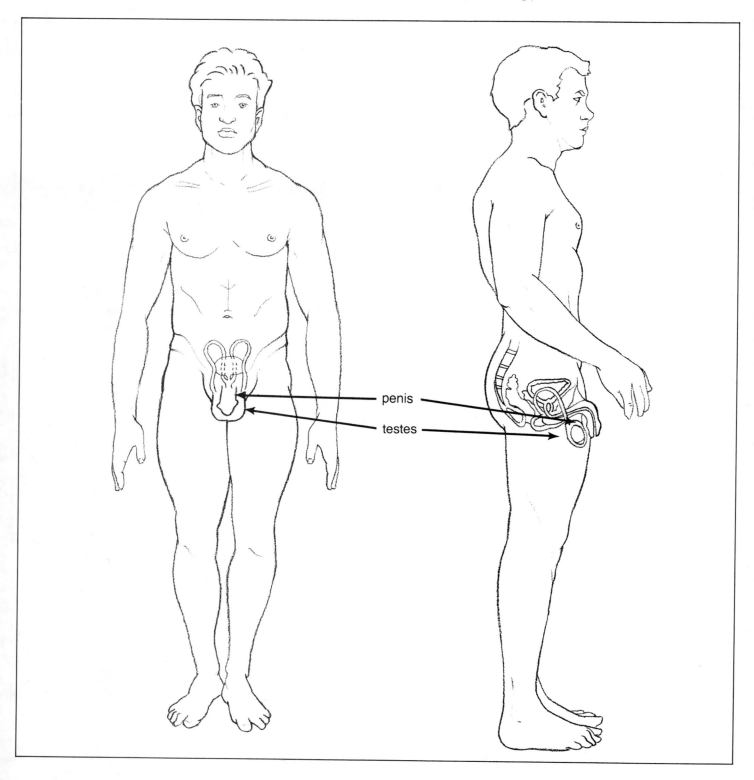

penis

testes

Getting pregnant

When you have intercourse (have sex, make love), the man puts his penis into your vagina. When the man "comes," the sperm in the semen go into your vagina. They swim through the cervix into your uterus. They make their way to the fallopian tubes.

If one sperm meets one egg in the fallopian tube, the sperm fertilizes the egg. The fertilized egg moves down the tube to the uterus. The egg starts to plant itself in the lining of the uterus. It starts to grow into a baby. You are pregnant.

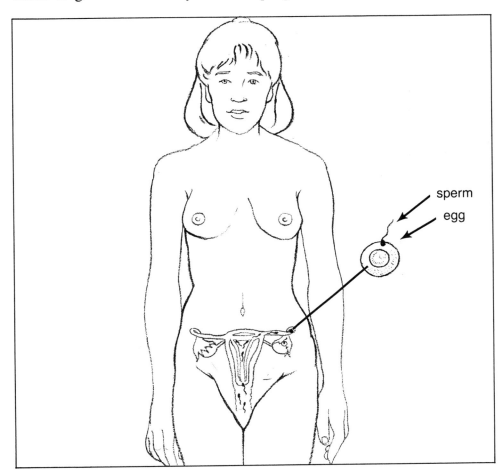

Signs of being pregnant:
- If you are pregnant, you will not get your period. (Sometimes you may get a light period. This is called spotting. Tell your doctor if you are spotting.)
- If you are pregnant, your breasts will feel full. Your nipples may seem bigger. Your bra may feel too tight.
- Some women feel sick when they are pregnant. You may throw up or feel like you want to throw up. This usually happens when you first wake up. It's often called "morning sickness." But the feeling can come at any time.
- You may feel very tired.
- You may need to go to the bathroom a lot.

Questions and answers about getting pregnant

Can you get pregnant the first time you have sex?
Yes.

I heard you can't get pregnant during your period. Is this true?
No. You can get pregnant if you have sex during your period.

Can you get pregnant if you don't "come"?
Yes. If an egg is in your fallopian tube, you can get pregnant.

How not to get pregnant

There are two basic ways not to get pregnant: don't have sex, or use birth control.

After you have your baby, you may not want to get pregnant again right away. If you have sex, you must use birth control. You can get pregnant even if you haven't had your period since your baby was born. You can get pregnant even if you are breast-feeding.

You may want to talk to your doctor or nurse about birth control. These are the most common forms. Some are more effective than others. You will have to decide which is best for you. The best method is one you will use, whether prescribed by a doctor or not.

Condoms, "Rubbers"

How does it work?
- fits over penis
- catches sperm when man comes

Strong points
- very effective
- easy to buy and use
- can be used by a man
- protects against STDs and AIDS

Weak points
- must be put on each time
- may irritate skin
- some men do not like them
- doesn't work as well on its own as some other methods

Diaphragm
(fitted by doctor)

How does it work?
- small rubber cap fits inside vagina; covers opening to uterus

Strong points
- use only when needed
- very effective when used with spermicide
- can put it in two hours before sex
- no side effects

Weak points
- can be messy
- takes time to learn to use it right
- must be left in place 6-8 hours so spermicide can work
- mother must be fitted for a new one after each baby is born

Spermicide
(foam, cream, jelly)

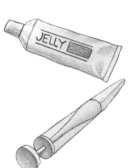

How does it work?
- put into vagina before sex
- made of chemical that kills sperm
- most effective when used with condom or diaphragm

Strong points
- easy to buy
- easy to use
- helps protect against STDs

Weak points
- must be put in 20 minutes or less before sex
- can be messy
- can irritate skin
- not as effective on its own as other methods

"The Pill"

(must be prescribed by doctor)

How does it work?
- Pill is made of hormones. Stops ovaries from releasing an egg each month.

Weak points
- may cause weight changes, mood swings
- must take it every day
- small chance of high blood pressure, heart attack, stroke, vaginal infections
- cannot take it when you are breast-feeding

Strong points
- easy to use
- does not interfere with lovemaking, regular periods

Sterilization

One other form of birth control is sterilization. Sterilization is an operation done by a doctor. It can be done on men and women (the operation for men is simpler).

Strong point
- no other method will ever be needed

Weak points
- permanent; you cannot change your mind
- small chance of infection after operation

Glossary

afterbirth
The placenta. It is delivered after the baby is born.

after pains
Pains you feel for a few days after the baby is born, as the uterus starts to shrink.

alcohol
A drug found in wine, beer, and cocktails. It should be avoided during pregnancy.

amniotic sac (am nee OT ik)
The bag of water that protects the baby inside the uterus.

anesthetic (an iss THET ik)
A drug that stops all feeling, including pain.

birth center
A place where women have babies. May or may not be part of a hospital.

birth control
Ways of preventing pregnancy.

birthing room
A room where a woman can go through labor and have her baby.

bladder
Organ of your body that holds urine.

bloody show
A sign that labor will start soon. The mucus plug that has sealed the cervix comes out.

breast-feed, breast-feeding
Nursing. Feeding your baby with milk from your own body.

caffeine (ka FEEN)
A drug found in coffee, tea, and some sodas. It should be avoided during pregnancy.

cervix (SIR viks)
The opening to the uterus.

cesarean (sih ZAIR ee un)
An operation to deliver a baby. A cut is made through the belly and uterus. The baby is lifted out of this opening.

circumcision (SIR kum SIZH un)
An operation often done on baby boys. The skin over the head of the penis is removed.

colostrum (KUH lah strum)
Baby's first food. Thin, white milk from your breasts.

condom
A birth control device. Worn by the man.

constipation
Hard, dry bowel movement.

contraction
A tightening of the muscles of the uterus.

convulsion
Severe, twitching fit. Eyes may roll back. Can be a sign of a serious health problem.

craving
Wanting only certain foods like ice cream or candy.

delivery room
The hospital room where most women have babies.

diabetes (DIE uh BEE teez)
A disease often called "sugar disease." Can cause serious problems in pregnancy. It can be treated.

diaphragm (DIE uh fram)
A birth control device. A woman inserts it into her vagina to block the cervix.

diarrhea (DIE uh REE uh)
Loose, runny bowel movements many times a day.

dilate
To open up. The cervix dilates during labor.

disposables
Diapers you can throw away.

douche
Product used to clean out the vagina.

dropping
The baby gets into position for birth. Sometimes called "engagement" or "lightening."

due date
The day you have figured your baby will be born. To find your due date, you need to know the date of your last period.

embryo (EM bree oh)
The baby during the first three months of pregnancy.

enema (EN uh muh)
Part of the "prep" done soon after you get to the hospital. Makes you have a bowel movement.

engagement

See *dropping*.

epidural (EP ih DER ul)

Anesthetic for labor and birth. You are awake but can't feel anything in the lower part of your body.

episiotomy (uh PEEZ ee OT uh mee)

A cut the doctor makes at the opening of the vagina before the baby is born.

fallopian tubes (fuh LOH pee un)

Connect the ovaries to the uterus.

false labor

Contractions that do not open the cervix.

fertilization

When an egg and sperm meet.

fetal monitor

Machine that shows the baby's heart rate.

fetus (FEET us)

Unborn baby; name used after the first three months of pregnancy.

formula

Milk for bottle-feeding the baby. It comes in a can.

helper

The person who will help you during labor and birth. Sometimes called a labor partner or coach.

hemorrhoids (HEM uh ROYDZ)

Painful, swollen veins, usually near the anus (the opening through which bowel movements pass).

hormones

Chemicals that control changes in your body.

intercourse

The act of having sex, making love.

I.V.

(*into a vein*) Lets medicine drip into your body through a vein in your hand.

kegel (KEE gul)

An exercise for your vagina.

labia (LAY bee uh)

The skin around the outside of your vagina.

labor

Stages your body goes through to have a baby.

labor room
Where women get ready for birth. Where they have their contractions before it is time to push the baby out.

lightening
See *dropping*.

lochia (LOH kee uh)
A vaginal discharge, like a period, after childbirth.

menstruation
Your period. The extra lining built up in your uterus comes out when you are not pregnant.

midwife
A person specially trained to help women during pregnancy and childbirth.

miscarriage
Pregnancy ends before the baby can live on its own. Most miscarriages happen in the first trimester.

natural childbirth
Birth without medicine.

navel
The belly button. Where the umbilical cord was attached to the baby.

nourishment
Food.

obstetrician (OB stuh TRISH un)
A doctor trained to treat pregnant women.

organ
A part of your body that does a certain job.

ovary, ovaries
Female sex organs. Produce eggs.

pediatrician (PEE dee uh TRISH un)
A doctor who cares for infants and children.

pelvic exam
Also called an internal exam. A doctor will check inside your vagina. The cervix is checked. (*Pelvic* refers to parts of the body near the pelvis.)

pelvic rock
An exercise to help get rid of a backache.

pelvis
Bones that support the baby during pregnancy; your hip bones.

penis (PEE nis)
 A man's sex organ. Releases sperm when the man "comes" during sex.

placenta (pluh SEN tuh)
 Organ that forms inside your uterus when you're pregnant. Sends blood and nourishment to the baby through the umbilical cord.

plug of mucus
 Closes the cervix when you are pregnant. Comes out during labor. See also *bloody show.*

postnatal
 After childbirth.

pregnancy
 The nine-month period when a baby grows inside your uterus.

pregnant
 Carrying an unborn baby.

premature birth
 When a baby is born too soon.

prenatal care
 Regular checkups while you are pregnant.

prep
 Preparing a woman for birth. The hair around the vagina is shaved and an enema is given.

protein
 An important part of your diet. You get protein from meat, fish, eggs, dried beans, etc.

puberty (PYOU ber tee)
 A growth period that usually occurs in the early teen years. When a boy reaches puberty, he is able to father a baby. When a girl reaches puberty, she is able to have a baby.

sedative
 Medicine to help you relax. Can be given during labor.

semen (SEE mun)
 Whitish liquid that contains sperm.

sonogram
 A picture of the baby inside the uterus, made by an ultrasound machine.

sperm
 Tiny cells found in a man's semen. When a man's sperm and a woman's egg meet during intercourse, an embryo is formed.

spermicide
 Made of chemicals that kill sperm.

spinal
Anesthetic for labor and birth. You are awake but can't feel anything in the lower part of your body.

spotting
A light discharge from the vagina. A little bit of blood, like a very light period.

STD
Sexually transmitted disease.

sterilization
An operation that makes a man or a woman unable to make a baby.

superstitions
Common beliefs that aren't true; "old wives' tales."

testes
Male sex organs where sperm are produced.

trimester
Three months. Pregnancy is divided into three trimesters.

ultrasound
A machine that lets the doctor see the baby inside the uterus. Gives a picture of how the baby is growing. See *sonogram*.

umbilical cord (um BIL ih kul)
The tube that connects the placenta to the baby. It carries blood and nourishment to the baby. See *navel*.

urine
Waste liquid; "pee" or "piss."

uterus (YOU ter us)
A strong muscle, sometimes called the womb. Your baby grows inside your uterus.

vagina (vuh JI nuh)
Passageway from the uterus. In childbirth, it's called the "birth canal." The baby is pushed out of the uterus and through the vagina.

vaginal discharge
Any liquid that comes out your vagina. Some discharges are sticky or thick.

varicose veins
Swollen painful veins, usually in the legs.

VBAC
Vaginal Birth After Cesarean.

vernex

Creamy coating on the skin of some newborns. Protects the baby's skin inside the uterus.

vitamins

Important part of a healthy diet. You can take special prenatal vitamins during pregnancy.

womb (woom)

Another name for the uterus.

Resources for the Teacher

Baby Care
> Samuels, Mike and Nancy. *The Well Baby Book.* New York: Simon and
> Schuster. 1979.

Breast-feeding
> Spangler, Amy. *A Practical Guide to Breast-feeding.* Available through
> APGBF, P.O. Box 71804, Marietta, Georgia, 30007.

Childbirth Education
> Hassid, Patricia. *Textbook for Childbirth Educators.* Philadelphia: J.B.
> Lippincott. 1984.
> Nichols, F. and Humenick, S. *Childbirth Education: Practice, Research, and
> Theory.* Philadelphia: W. B. Saunders. 1988.

Exercise
> Holstein, Barbara. *Shaping Up for a Healthy Pregnancy.* Human Kinetics
> Press, Box 5076, Champaign, Illinois, 61820.

Maternal Child Health Resources
> *Starting Early: A Guide to Federal Resources in Maternal Child Health,*
> National Maternal Child Health Clearinghouse (NMCHCH), 38th and R
> Street, N.W., Washington, D.C., 20057

Nutrition
> *Food for the Teenager During and After Pregnancy,* U.S. Department of Health
> and Human Services, Division of Maternal and Child Health, Rockville,
> Maryland, 20857. #82-5106.

Preterm Labor
> *Preterm Labor: Its Management and Diagnosis,* The March of Dimes Birth
> Defects Foundation, Professional Education Department, 1275
> Mamaroneck Avenue, White Plains, New York, 10605.

Substance Abuse
> *National Prevention Network Directory,* National Clearinghouse on Alcohol
> and Drug Information, P.O. Box 2345, Rockville, Maryland, 20852.

Sudden Infant Death Syndrome (SIDS)
> National SIDS Clearinghouse, 8201 Greensboro Drive, Suite 600, McLean,
> Virginia, 22102.

Teacher Training
> Perinatal Health and Fitness Network (PHFN), 227 Scottholm Terrace,
> Syracuse, New York, 13224.

Teaching Relaxation
> Jones, Carl. *Visualizations for an Easier Childbirth.* New York: Simon and
> Schuster. 1988.

Women's Health
> *The New Our Bodies, Ourselves,* The Boston's Women's Health Book
> Collective, New York: Simon and Schuster. 1984.

Index

M

making love *see* sexual intercourse
male sex organs, 92
maternity clothes, 17
maternity leave, 36, 42
medicine, 20, 23, 29, 35
    baby's, 87
    during labor, 49, 65, 66, 67
    while breast-feeding, 81
    while pregnant, 14
menstruation *see also* monthly period, 90
midwife, 23, 25
miscarriage, 28, 29
MMR shot, 87
monthly period, 20, 21, 90, 93, 94
morning sickness, 28, 93

N

natural childbirth, 50, 63-64
navel *see* belly button
newborn, 75

O

obstetrician *see also* doctor, mother's, 18
old wives' tales *see* superstitions
ovaries, 90-91, 96

P

pediatrician *see also* doctor, baby's, 87
pelvic exam, 19, 23, 54, 64
penis, 92, 93, 94
pill, birth control, 71, 96
pins and needles, 32
placenta, 27, 60, 61
planning
    for baby, 15, 29, 42, 43
    for childbirth, 36
    to go to hospital, 42
plug of mucus, 27, 46
polio shots, 87
postnatal care
    baby's, 87-88
    mother's, 69
pregnancy
    how it happens, 90-94
    preventing, 94-96
    signs of, 93
premature birth, 40
prenatal care, 11, 18-23
    cost of, 22
    first appointment, 19-21
    making appointments, 21-22
prep, 56
puberty, 90

R

"rubbers" *see* condom
rubella, 20

S

sanitary napkins, 69
school, 15, 17, 38
sedative, 49, 65
semen, 92
sex *see* sexual intercourse
sex organs
    female, 90-91
    male, 92
sexual intercourse (making love, sex), 46, 47, 93, 94
    after pregnancy, 71
    during pregnancy, 29
shots, baby's, 87
show *see* bloody show
"showing," 17, 30
side pains, 32
skin
    baby's, 58, 86
    mother's, 35
sleep
    baby's, 75
    mother's, 34
smoking, 14, 15, 16, 29, 40, 79
    and breast-feeding, 80
soft spot, 39
sonogram, 23
sperm, 27, 93, 94
spermicide, 95
spinal anesthetic, 49, 65
spitting up, 86
spotting, 93
STD (sexually transmitted disease), 20, 29, 61, 94, 95
sterilization, 96
stretch marks, 35
superstitions, 35, 36

T

tampons, 69
testes, 92
thrush, 86
toxoplasmosis, 17
travel during pregnancy, 35
trimester, 24
trimester, first, 24-29
    problems in, 28
    things to do in, 29
trimester, second, 30-36
    problems in, 32
    things to do in, 36

trimester, third, 37-43
    problems in, 40
    things to do in, 42-43

U

ultrasound, 23, 67
umbilical cord, 27, 60, 61, 86
urine
    after pregnancy, 71
    sample of, 19, 23
uterus, 19, 23, 24, 27, 47, 69, 90-91, 93

V

vagina, 19, 35, 91, 93, 95
    pains in, 41
vaginal discharge, 32, 40
varicose veins, 41
venereal disease *see also* STD, 20, 61
vernex, 58
vitamins, 17

W

warning signs in third trimester, 40
weight gain during pregnancy, 17, 23
weight loss after pregnancy, 69
work, 15, 17, 36

X

X rays, 23

Other books for parents from New Readers Press:

A Good Beginning: Enjoying your baby's first year

When a Baby Is New

As a Child Grows

Let's Work It Out: Topics for Parents

Family Reading

The Long and Short of Mother Goose

Favorite Childhood Tales